SETTING THE SCENE

SETTING THE SCENE

A Garden Design Masterclass
from Repton to the Modern Age

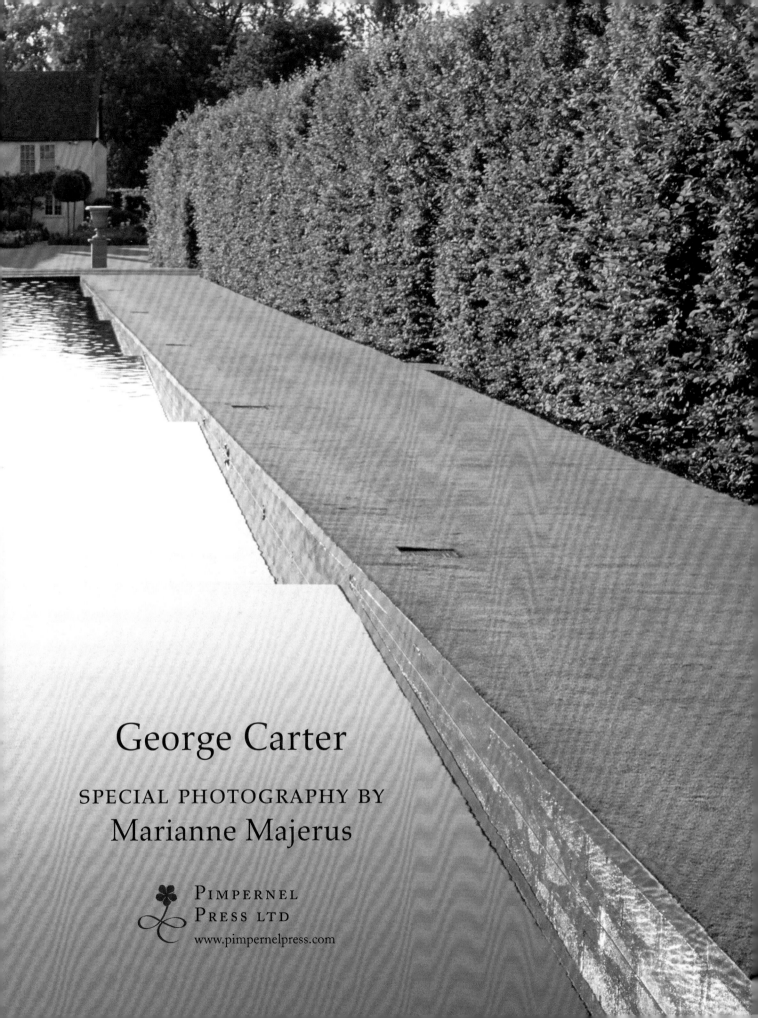

George Carter

SPECIAL PHOTOGRAPHY BY
Marianne Majerus

PIMPERNEL
PRESS LTD
www.pimpernelpress.com

Pimpernel Press Limited
www.pimpernelpress.com

SETTING THE SCENE
A Garden Design Masterclass from Repton to the Modern Age

Designed by Anne Wilson
Typeset in Gauthier and Aldus

ISBN 978-1-910258-59-0

Printed and bound in China
by C&C Offset Printing Company Limited

987654321

HALF TITLE PAGE Vignette from Humphry Repton's
Theory and Practice of Landscape Gardening (1803)
TITLE PAGE The cascade at Tilbury Hall
THESE PAGES The Green Theatre at Silverstone Farm

CONTENTS

PREFACE

IN THIS BOOK I have distilled a career of more than thirty years in garden design and a varied series of projects all over the world into nuggets that I hope will be useful to others. These ideas can be applied to gardens of all sizes. My work has been inspired by the gardens of the past, from the formality of the sixteenth and seventeenth centuries to the informal landscapes of the eighteenth and nineteenth centuries. The work and writings of the prolific landscape designer Humphry Repton (1752–1818) have been a major inspiration.

Repton presented his ideas to clients under various headings and in the form of bound volumes - his famous 'Red Books'. They formed the basis of his four influential works on gardening and landscaping: *Sketches and Hints on Landscape Gardening* (1795); *Observations on the Theory and Practice of Landscape Gardening* (1803); *An Inquiry into Changes of Taste in Landscape Gardening* (1806); and *Fragments on the Theory and Practice of Landscape Gardening* (with J. A. Repton, 1816). His mixture of aesthetic theory and practical advice, backed up by reasoned argument, has strongly influenced modern landscape design. Here I have used similar headings and many of the same ideas to draw together my own approach to garden design based on projects of widely different type and scale over a long period.

LEFT George Carter at work in the barn at Silverstone Farm.
ABOVE Repton's trade card, engraved by Thomas Medland in 1788 after a design by Repton, was pasted into all his Red Books throughout his career. It illustrated his surveying skills and the scale of landscape he aspired to design. He coined the term 'landscape gardener'.

The Red Book for Brandsbury, 1789, illustrated proposals for the 100-acre landscape of a villa now swallowed up by the North London suburb of Willesden. Repton illustrated his improvements in this graphic manner - a paper flap can be lifted to show the 'rich distances' that could be revealed by the removal of an existing fence.

I also often present my proposals adapting Repton's invention the 'before' and 'after' view, using a photograph rather than a watercolour of the 'before' or existing view, shown in contrast to a watercolour visual as the 'after'. The combination of these views, together with a ground plan, makes it easier for clients to understand the proposals.

The basis of Repton's work was the then fashionable theory of the Picturesque. This aesthetic theory radically altered the way the British looked at their own natural landscape, and this in turn informed the way that parks and gardens were designed and appreciated. So much was written about the aesthetics of landscape in the late eighteenth century that any moderately well-read layman could have made an intelligent attempt at appreciating and deconstructing a piece of scenery, natural or artificial, either in a picture or in real life. Many of the educated public were both ready and anxious to improve their own country or suburban property, however small, on picturesque principles. Uvedale Price, William Gilpin, Richard Payne Knight and, to a lesser extent, Repton (who added a practical dimension to their ideas) were required reading, so that, armed with their advice and strictures, it was possible for the amateur to make a creditable attempt at designing his or her own garden or landscape. Taste in gardens and landscape was one of the obsessions of the age and vital to your social standing. The lack of such a lively debate on landscape design in the present age is one of the deficiencies of gardening today. Even the intelligent debate on sustainability can hardly be said to make up for the much wider-ranging interests of Repton's era.

Repton had the view that a garden

is an artificial object, and has no other pretence to be natural, than what it derives from the growth of the plants that adorn it; their selection, their disposition, their culture, must all be the work of art, and instead of that invisible line, or hidden fence - which separates the mown lawn from the lawn fed by cattle - it is more rational to shew that the two objects are separated, if the fence is not unsightly - otherwise, we must suppose that cattle are admitted to crop the flowers and shrubs or that flowers and shrubs are absurdly planted in a pasture exposed to cattle. (*An Inquiry*, 1806)

The addition of practical ideas to the aesthetic of picturesque theory marked Repton out, and it is this aspect of his work that makes it so appealing and valuable today. I have often lamented that the nearly universal rules of taste formulated in the eighteenth century have no real modern equivalent. The pattern books based on classical theory (however flexibly interpreted) produced by architects and writers ensured an almost universal standard of good building even down to the humblest structures, and the same can be said of the effect that the literature on gardens produced in the same period. Although there is no shortage of publications on both subjects today, there seems to be a lack of simple pattern books and sound theory that might produce a similarly broad standard of good design. You could speculate that TV gardening has had a similar effect, and indeed it has improved general knowledge, but it seems not to have taught the practical and aesthetic lessons that are embedded in garden history and that offer such a useful resource to today's garden designers and makers.

It is true to say that you cannot take any area of study forward without understanding its history. You throw away so many stimulating ideas and theories by failing to look closely at the past. The ancient Romans, for instance, had a particularly modern sensibility towards gardens and landscapes, appreciating both the wild and the manicured, as well as the interesting contrasts that can be achieved by juxtaposing the two. One of the inspirations for the development of the landscape garden in Britain in the early eighteenth century was a book commissioned by Lord Burlington, Robert Castell's *The Villas of the Ancients Illustrated* (1728). This book interpreted Pliny's descriptions of the gardens and landscapes of his own villas in graphic form, imagining them as a careful contrast of the wild against the formal.

If my work can be said to have a style it must be one created from an amalgam of the ideas of the past - not as a pastiche but as a synthesis, making something new. I have not ignored modernism, now a historical style as well as a philosophy. Its development in the early twentieth century was much inspired by early nineteenth-century pared-down classicism, and it is this aspect that appeals to me.

Using Repton as its inspiration, this book is organized under the headings that a Red Book might have contained, and shows how most of these ideas are still relevant today, even when gardens are in the main much reduced in scale.

INTRODUCTION

It has been objected to the mode in which I deliver my plans,
that they do not always convey instructions, sufficiently clear,
to act as guide to the detail of execution.

INTRODUCTION TO THE RED BOOK FOR
BLAISE CASTLE, BRISTOL, 1796

T HE RED BOOK was intended to give an overview of a site, together with
some suggested general ideas. It was not conceived as an in-depth guide for
a contractor to use as working drawings, although the plan, descriptive text and
sketches are often very specific. Repton's introductions often give a short account
of his visit. They sum up the client's brief or general wishes, and give a précis of
his immediate impressions. You can also deduce from this introductory text how
Repton evaluated the client: their knowledge of gardening and farming, for instance,
is indicated by how much he chose to say about general principles - spelling out to
some what might be self-evident to others. This brief preamble is useful in that it sets
the tone and scope for the whole project.

Repton almost never discussed money at this point - or ever, really - in explicit
terms in the Red Books. (An exception to this is the Red Book for Welbeck Abbey for
the Duke of Portland, where at the duke's request he costed some of his suggestions.)
His client probably knew his hourly rate in advance of a visit: this sum varied as his
career progressed. His fees are famously discussed in Jane Austen's *Mansfield Park*,
written between 1811 and 1813, where they are stated to be five guineas a day plus
expenses, though by that date his fees are known to have been related to the distance
he had to travel - then a very expensive and slow process. If he had to travel within
one stage of London (one day's ride or carriage drive), the first visit was charged at
ten guineas, up to a hundred miles fifty guineas, and so on. The overall budget for
implementing his suggestions would, however, generally have been an unknown
quantity, and many of Repton's ideas were costly. Earth-moving, for instance, was
a much more expensive operation in the late eighteenth century than it is today.
Repton did not confine himself to the landscape, and often recommended radical

Humphry Repton, engraved frontispiece to *Observations on*
the Theory and Practice of Landscape Gardening (1803).

changes to a house's layout or elevation, and even its complete re-siting or rebuilding. He realized that houses and gardens are interrelated, and that it is often as important to deal with the shortcomings of a house as it is to improve its setting.

Because Repton did not have his own contracting team it would have been difficult, from a Red Book only, for a client to determine what the proposals were likely to cost, and it must have been a bit of a dive into the unknown to consider implementing the many ideas that the average Red Book throws out. Now, however, it is essential to discuss an outline budget and timescale for works at an early stage - topics that hardly any Red Book addresses. Often schemes, then as now, were designed to be carried out in stages over a long period as funds and time permitted. Only occasionally are large private gardens set out, built and planted in their entirety in one go; Repton called this rare circumstance 'a creation'.

A Red Book was designed to inspire his client, not to provide specific instructions. The fine detail, if required, was delivered on site at a later date. You can usually tell from the brief Introduction what Repton decided the principal issues were. He used it to signal the scope of his proposals - sometimes quite modest, at other times very elaborate and complicated.

OPPOSITE, ABOVE Lamer House, Hertfordshire, 1792, from the Red Book 'before' view. Repton disliked the effect of red brick buildings in a landscape.

OPPOSITE, BELOW Lamer House from the Red Book 'after' view, showing the house washed a stone colour and with the addition of a pediment and a tripartite sash window above the front door.

BELOW White Lodge, Richmond Park, London. Repton advised Lord Sidmouth in 1805 on what he called this 'modern villa', and suggested a formal flower garden rather seventeenth century in character between the house and park. He thought this a more functional and useful arrangement than the previous one, where 'troublesome animals of every kind' grazed right up to the house.

The south front of Silverstone Farm, Norfolk, a modest farmhouse actually built in 1920, though not dissimilar from local farmhouses built a century or more earlier. The pleasing symmetry is enhanced by a few simple refinements, including narrower first-floor windows and a brick string course between ground and first floors. The formal garden has been designed to axis on the front door.

In my work each project has its own scale. Some are large, while others, such as London gardens, may be small but complicated. The smaller the space, the more considered the detail has to be. A few case studies from my work illustrate the large and the small, the simple and the complex. My range is perhaps wider than Repton might have tackled, though he did undertake small projects for friends as well as the large-scale parks of his richer clients. The smaller houses for which he produced schemes include his own cottage at Hare Street, near Romford, Essex, a four-bedroomed cottage on the High Road, and the Rectory, Lyng, Norfolk, a modest three-bay house with a small riverside garden.

My own garden at Silverstone Farm in Norfolk is two acres in extent and has been developed over twenty-five years. It is necessarily simple, as the maintenance has to be kept low for reasons of both time and cost. Influenced as it is by late seventeenth- and early eighteenth-century

European gardens, it is about as far as you can get from Repton's own aesthetic, but nevertheless I have borrowed many elements in it from him. These will appear in the chapters to which they relate, but for the purpose of this introductory section I should say that I have borne in mind that the house, a modest farmhouse, sets the tone for the garden in that the detailing and materials are very simple. A farmhouse, however, is a type of building that Repton would not have countenanced for his clients. He was always very keen to make sure that their houses should not be mistaken for farmhouses - clearly not suitable dwellings in the late eighteenth century for persons of taste. Paradoxically, a 'cottage' as a building type could be countenanced, so long as it had been suitably elevated to a *cottage orné*.

Silverstone Farm has in places a sense of grandeur of scale, but I hope it nowhere strays into the inappropriately grand. And I hope Repton would think that it suits the modest income and status of its owner.

Repton's cottage at Hare Street, near Romford, Essex. Repton dressed this modest farmhouse on a village street to have the character of a *cottage orné*, using treillage supporting striped awnings, probably of canvas. The house has disappeared but the site is still identifiable. He moved here in 1786-7 from Norfolk and lived in the house until his death in 1818. This miniature engraving by John Peltro appeared in *The Polite Repository for 1805*. Repton used this almanac as a way of advertising his work, supplying annually twelve or more views of places where he had given advice.

He described his own home at Hare Street, an outer London hamlet in Essex, as 'this humble cottage to which for more than forty years I have anxiously retreated from the pomp of palaces, the elegancies of fashion and the allurements of dissipation' (Fragment XXXVI, *Fragments*, 1816). At Hare Street he managed to scale down his ideas to suit a house in a village street. It is one of the very few instances we have of his detailed views on a size of house and grounds more in line with those of today.

Wood Hall is an Elizabethan House for which Repton presented a Red Book in February 1807. His proposals included a large oval walled kitchen garden to the west of the house, and I was asked to undertake the simplification of this area in 1995. This garden had already undergone a radical change of use, in that its potentially vast vegetable and fruit

A formal vista created within the Repton walled garden of Wood Hall in Norfolk. The garden, unusually, is oval in plan. The splayed pleached hornbeam hedges create a screen to hide a tennis court on the right. The underscaled facade at the apex is designed to increase the apparent depth of the site and is axised on an old glasshouse against a south-facing wall.

production was no longer needed. It now houses an ornamental garden of borders and nut walks, a tennis court (which had to be concealed) and two remaining glasshouses. Comparatively close to the house, it comprises the main gardening activity of the whole site, the rest of which remains parkland with a strong Reptonian feel. Its walls and orientation to the south make it the warmest and most comfortable part of the garden.

King's College Library in Chancery Lane, London, is a Gothic Revival building of *c*.1820, originally the Public Record Office. Its one-acre site was redesigned as a garden for the users of the library when it was converted by the University in 2001. The garden had to be very simple both to install and to maintain. It uses the paradoxical idea that a space appears larger when it is subdivided and when the boundaries are concealed (an idea propounded

King's College Library garden, London. A large open space, in a built-up part of central London, has been subdivided by hornbeam hedges to create separate outdoor rooms for library users. The main entrances of the early nineteenth-century Gothic Revival building dictated the axes that run through the enclosed spaces. Existing trees were retained and incorporated into the design.

by the poet Alexander Pope in 1731 and taken up later by Repton). A restrained layout of hornbeam-hedged enclosures contains seats, pools and sculpture. The axes created by openings in the hedges relate to the building and form vistas that frame the 'incidents' within the outdoor rooms. Existing mature trees were retained and are also 'framed' by the geometry of the hedges.

The Garden of Surprises at Burghley House, in Lincolnshire, makes a marked contrast to these simple gardens. A completely new garden deliberately designed for visitors, it has no relationship to the house and is therefore a work in itself - inward-looking and self-contained. Lady Victoria Leatham very much wanted to create some reference to the garden made by the Cecils (who built Burghley) at Theobalds, Hertfordshire, in the late sixteenth and early seventeenth centuries. This garden was lost in the 1650s but is well known from contemporary descriptions. In its day Theobalds was one of Britain's most famous gardens: in fact, James I liked it so much that he obliged Robert Cecil, Earl of Salisbury, to swap it for Hatfield. Its particular feature was the inventive use of water in fountains, moats and canals, and this dominance of water was my main inspiration for the Garden of Surprises, which comprises a series of water jokes, grottoes and automata linked by a formal structure of green rooms.

OPPOSITE A curtain of water forms the exit 'gate' at the Garden of Surprises. It is linked to a sensor that shuts down the jets as you approach the exit. Tufa gate piers frame the jets. One of the existing Elizabethan-style stone gateways inspired the topiary surround framing the public entrance gate to the garden.

BELOW The jet garden looking towards a multi-purpose sundial designed by William Andrews, and beyond that to the column at the centre of the maze.

Repton was attuned to historic styles and at various sites recreated gardens in a sixteenth- or seventeenth-century manner – mainly led by the style and date of the house to which they related. He was also good at assembling several historical elements in a single garden, as at Ashridge in Hertfordshire (see page 118), where different medieval monastic features were put together to make a series of interlinked incidents.

Penshurst Place in Kent has a large garden long open to the public with a geometric layout that still reflects the seventeenth-century garden plan depicted by Johannes Kip and Jan Knyff in their bird's-eye view of 1719. This garden has undergone many changes in its detailing and planting schemes since then, but broadly its plan remains the same. I have been making minor changes since the 1990s, but one major recent change has been the replanting of the long (275-foot) double mixed border, which had its first appearance in this form in about 1900. The garden was considered 'old-fashioned' at that date and was much admired for that reason by Gertrude Jekyll and William Robinson and by the Edwardian watercolourists Beatrice Parsons and George Samuel Elgood, who both painted it.

An early eighteenth-century bird's-eye view of Penshurst Place, Kent, engraved by Johannes Kip for John Harris's *History of Kent*, shows the garden with broadly the same layout as survives today. The double herbaceous borders opposite are on the line of the walk shown in the centre of this detail to the right of the house.

The borders are designed as five distinct colour-themed bays divided by grass indents that both reduce the maintenance and provide neutral respites between the different colour schemes. The colours move from hot red in the foreground to cool blue in the distance, with orange-yellow and purple in between. This redesign of the border has one characteristic that is taken directly from Repton: his use of colour in planting to imitate or enhance aerial perspective – the idea that landscapes naturally appear bluer and greyer in the distance through the optical effect of tiny particles of dust trapped in the atmosphere. As a landscape painter he took advantage of this phenomenon to give increased depth to his watercolours. He also suggested that strident or hot colours only had a place in the foreground of a scene. Used in the middle or far distance they would break up the sense of a continued recession that he thought key to a satisfactory view. To this end strong colours are only seen in the foreground of his landscapes – either in the pleasure grounds immediately next to the house, or in the separate formal flower garden which would have little place in the landscape at large.

The newly replanted long herbaceous borders at Penshurst are arranged in five bays, each with its own colour scheme. They move from red in the foreground, through orange, yellow and purple, ending with blue in the distance. Each section is insulated from the next by an indent of lawn flanked by blocks of box.

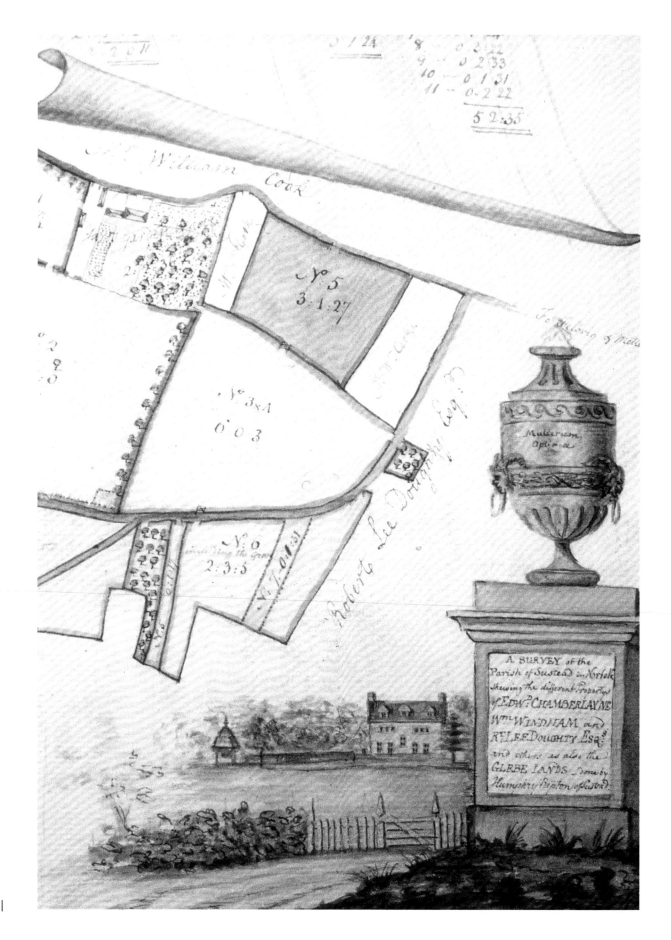

PLAN

I have frequently observed, that those who perfectly understand a drawing in perspective, have, sometimes, no idea of a plan or map, and are not ashamed to confess they do not understand either.

FRAGMENT XXV, *FRAGMENTS*, 1816

I N A RED BOOK the plan, normally a full-page coloured sketch, is the key reference to the whole site and appears early in the sequence. Repton realized that a plan conveys little to a general audience, and his great step forward was to supplement the plan with a series of watercolour perspective views that clearly show what the plan would look like from various points of view - a distinct advance on Capability Brown, who only presented his ideas as plans. The modern designer can present the same information as perspective visuals, drawn or digital, contrasted against photographs of the existing site. This can be supplemented by axonometric visuals or by a bird's-eye view which can be extrapolated from an aerial photograph or drone image.

Today - now that topographical surveys are much more accurate - the plan has infinitely greater sophistication. The modern garden designer also has more information readily to hand to describe a site - aerial and ground photography, satellite imagery, modern and historical Ordnance Survey maps and highly accurate digital surveys. Repton often commissioned a survey from a professional surveyor, but for smaller projects he drew a sketch plan himself or relied on crude existing estate maps as a basis for his own.

The plan enabled Repton - as it does designers today - to plot the principal elements of a design: the contours, the drives and walks, water, the orientation of the house and broad planting schemes. Today a plan is developed in two or more phases: the first, like Repton's, outlines the main ideas suggested, and this is subsequently developed into an accurate guide for a contractor, giving dimensions, materials, drainage and electrics, detailed planting plans and hard landscaping. The Repton plan is of more use to the client than to the contractor. It is to a small scale (usually unstated), often encompassing the entire park within a standard format of about

Detail of a survey of the parish of Sustead, Norfolk, by Humphry Repton, with a vignette of the garden front of Repton's house, Sustead Old Hall, *c.*1745.

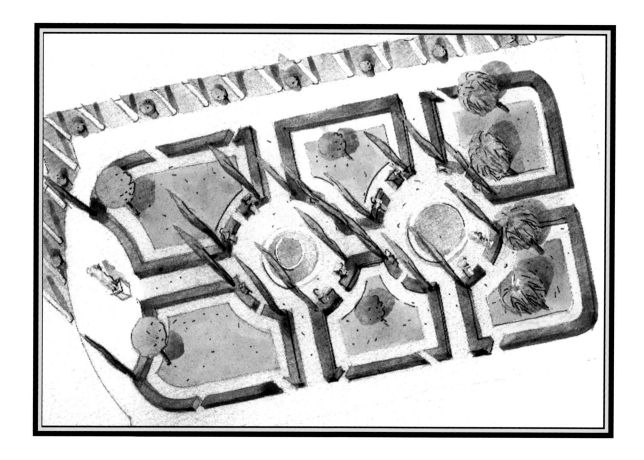

Villa Massimo, Rome: an isometric view showing the recasting of the existing parterre in an internal courtyard to relate to the building and to accommodate in a more considered way the scattered antiquities.

8½ x 11½ inches, so the information it contains is necessarily limited. There is often, however, useful maintenance information such as an indication of 'dressed lawn' or 'feeding lawn': mown or grazed grass.

Realizing that plans convey very little of the intended effect to a reader without professional expertise, Repton reproduced fewer plans than perspectives in his published works. Yet today the plan is of overriding importance to the garden designer's scheme, and much less emphasis is placed on perspective information. I prefer to use both, and generally produce rapid watercolour sketches to show the various intended effects. These help to refine the plan, since you can check as you go along whether what looks good in a plan will work in reality. Watercolours are, I find, more appealing than the most sophisticated digital visualizations, which, unless they are handled very expertly, tend towards a feeble aridity. The level of finish is generally dependent on the scope of the project: on the whole, the larger the project the more finished the view.

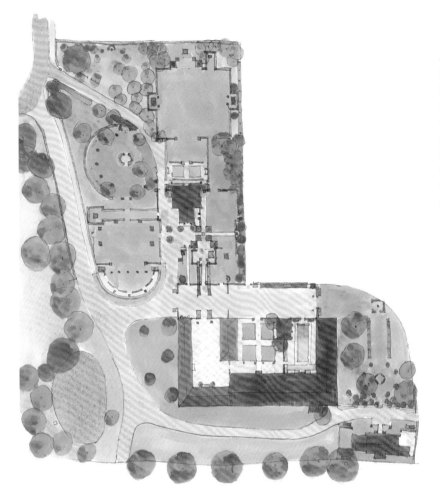

A plan (left) and an aerial photograph (below) of the garden at Silverstone Farm, Norfolk. The plan shows that the main axes of the garden are centred on the buildings and are pushed to the full limits of the site. Part of the point of this all-green architectural garden is the contrast of different kinds of space – open against closed, shaded against sunny.

CHARACTER

In deciding on the character of a place, some attention must be given to its situation with respect to other places; to the natural shape of the ground on which the house is, or may be, built; to the style and size of the house, and even to the rank of its possessor, together with the use which he intends to make of it.

SKETCHES AND HINTS, 1795

T HE CHARACTER OF A SITE - what was, in the eighteenth century, famously called the 'Genius of the Place'- is still key to the creation of gardens. The elements that determine character are the soil type and topography, the house and its architectural style, the climate and aspect. These characteristics apply to both urban and rural sites. Even a raw urban plot has its own intrinsic character that an enquiring designer and client will draw out or reveal. The type of site or style of building might suggest a predominantly formal or informal approach to design.

For Repton, to describe the character of a place was also to put it into a precise social position, and at the same time to categorize the wealth and aspirations of his client. If the site or house, as it was found, did not correctly reinforce this perceived position, then it could be altered to suit. Repton would be quite frank about telling a client that, for instance, farming in the foreground of a scene was not appropriate to a gentleman's residence. He would have spent some time telling him (for it was usually a man) what was the appropriate character for his house - this was an important starting point, which set the tone for everything else.

This concern with a setting not being quite appropriate to a certain social aspiration is not now an openly stated aim of garden design, though there might still be elements that could be read in this way. It is certainly true that some stylistic constraint is a great help in concentrating the mind and informing the design process. The types of house that Repton describes as needing a specific sort of setting are still to some extent relevant. He listed the following: a ducal palace (the 'feudal home' at the centre of a vast estate); a country house

The Royal Hospital, Chelsea, a view of the South Terrace - a series of grass terraces punctuated by gravel walks and yew pyramids. This recent redesign has opened up the view of the building from the river and provided a simple geometric foreground, much as its architect, Christopher Wren, envisaged it.

(the permanent residence of a landowner); a sporting seat (the occasional retreat of a sportsman); a villa (the weekend retreat of a merchant); a cottage (the spruced-up, modest but picturesque home of a person of taste). All of these types still exist and to some extent would still dictate an individual type and style of setting. There are additions to this canon of which Repton would not have approved: he would not have thought a farmhouse could become a residence of taste, nor would he have had much interest in the design of an urban terraced house garden, though larger town houses might have been worthy of his notice. Today the most common types would definitely include the old rectory and the country cottage, and both of these conjure up a style of garden that even the most hard-line modernist designer would not entirely ignore.

The style of an existing building is the next factor to be considered in determining character, and for Repton there was quite a range to be looked at and appraised. What he described as the elegant simplicity of the 'Grecian' style was perhaps his favourite. These are often astylar (that is, with no order of columns) but are classical in proportion and in the detail of mouldings. This style is perhaps the closest to modernism in that it largely eschews decoration and relies on material and three-dimensional form for its effect. Many of these houses exist and are still being built today, especially in the United States, where simple classicism remains a popular style, often carried out well by jobbing builders and developers without the advice of architects, much as they were in the eighteenth century. Such a house, according to Repton, defines the character of the setting as also 'elegantly simple' - perhaps with a little formality near the house, which gradually gives way to an unforced naturalism in the background.

Wilder, more picturesque scenery would not be appropriate to such a house, but it might be just what

is needed around a cottage (which in Repton's day could be quite a large house dressed up as a cottage). The nature of cottage architecture - irregular in plan and profile, of organic growth and of mixed, often rough-hewn materials - lends itself to a more complex style of gardening in which a variety of different incidents can be fitted around the loose and irregular plan.

Repton was also early in defining historic styles of architecture, and these too give a clue as to what kind of garden is appropriate. He saw 'Gothic', 'Castle' and 'Elizabethan' as distinct styles - whether in fact actually old or modern re-creations. To these he added 'Hindoo', 'Chinese' and 'Rustic' as potential patterns, each again requiring a particular type of setting, using historic gardens as an inspiration but given a particular Reptonian updated twist.

Finally, character is also determined crucially by the type of natural landscape within which the house is set. This factor is perhaps more in line with the approach of modern designers, who like to think their skill is to provide an update on Pope's 'Epistle to Lord Burlington' (1731): 'In all let Nature never be forgot. Consult the Genius of the Place in all.' This is easier to determine when the site is in the country surrounded by open landscape. But even confined urban spaces have underlying characteristics to do with soil type, aspect, climate, prospect and architectural style.

Repton's views on character are always pragmatic: all these factors affect the design of the grounds. It is interesting that in the quote at the beginning of this chapter he refers to neighbouring properties first - even in a far less populated Britain, the idea of the borrowed landscape of your neighbours, as well as the impact of their house and park on your own, was an important factor. He was very aware that it is no good trying to upstage a ducal neighbour's landscape. In an era of wide interest in the status conferred by land and the taste that is applied to it, you needed to be careful to modulate the setting

of the house to reinforce your social position and aesthetic sensibility.

The issue of the existing land forms was also important: a house built in the bottom of a valley would have to be treated quite differently from one on the top of a hill. Historic houses are often in valley bottoms, but even though Repton thought this could be gloomy and lacking in prospect, he did not necessarily suggest rebuilding on higher ground - it might be possible to make the best of such a site by making it more picturesque and cheerful.

The scale of a house was then - and is now - one of the principal considerations in deciding on the character of its setting. However the 'use' of a house and garden, which Repton mentions in passing, is perhaps a more important consideration today, when houses are often occupied as weekend retreats or as occasional holiday homes and have therefore to be treated in a much simpler and less labour-intensive

way than a permanent residence. The character of the architecture is still perhaps the most important factor in setting the scene, and though there might now be more categories of building style than Repton would have known, the material and architectural form of a house still dictate what is appropriate in planting and garden architecture.

Three houses created on the ramparts of the Spanish town of Trujillo by Juan and Annabel Garton. These were built on the remaining footprint of structures that looked across a vast panoramic landscape towards Portugal. The small gardens create a foreground to this view and look over the castellated town wall. The forms of the building and the shapes of the garden terraces are totally dictated by the rocky outcrops on which the town is built.

LARGE COUNTRY HOUSES

When the artificial magnificent style of geometric gardening of Le Nôtre was changed to the more natural style of landscape gardening, it often happened that too little respect was paid to the costly appendages of English Palaces: . . . to place a palace in the middle of a grass field, was one of those excesses of innovation to which all kinds of reform are liable. (*Changes of Taste,* 1806)

I HAVE WORKED AT SEVERAL LARGE COUNTRY HOUSES, and when I come to analyse them, they all have very different characters, mostly depending on the date and style of architecture and the landscapes within which they are set. One of my early jobs was at Holkham Hall in Norfolk (which was also one of Repton's earliest commissions). The project mainly involved simplifying and replanting parts of the William Andrews Nesfield parterre on the south front (1849 and after), the approach to it from the east, and the pleasure ground behind this approach. I also had the interesting commission of creating a temporary installation in straw near to the William Kent obelisk of 1719 (see also pages 200 and 201).

The element here that perhaps uses Reptonian theory most successfully is the series of yew pyramids that I planted against the house on the upper south grass terrace. They are intended to make a visual link between the Nesfield parterre and the colossal house, which is perched above the large retained terrace that Nesfield had to construct in order to gain enough flat ground for a parterre big enough for such a grand house. Their position relates both to the bays of the architecture and to the parterres themselves, and I think they make a suitable green link between the rather austere building and the complicated pattern of the parterres, urns and other sculptural ornament. Repton would perhaps have thought that they contributed a much-needed vertical foreground frame to the horizontal sweep of the parterre.

EVERY HOUSE AND GARDEN OF SOME AGE is a palimpsest of different dates, and all the layers of time have to be respected equally. However much you may wish that one layer could be peeled back to reveal another, this is seldom possible or even desirable. Much time can be spent in trying to achieve that very Reptonian concept, the compromise. One layer might be suppressed in order to reveal another, or invisible underlayers might be referred to in a subtle way. This is particularly the case at

OPPOSITE, ABOVE A construction using straw bales, at Holkham Hall, Norfolk. This temporary installation, commissioned to celebrate British Food and Farming Year in 1989, was designed to refer to the now overlaid Kent landscape on the south lawn.

OPPOSITE, BELOW The introduction of yew pyramids on the upper level of the Nesfield terrace at Holkham Hall is designed to make a visual link between the architecture and the parterre below.

Somerleyton Hall, Suffolk, which appears at a glance totally mid-Victorian, but is actually an encasement and overlay of an early seventeenth-century house and garden. This early garden was in fact one of the most famous, elaborate and up-to-date in East Anglia, as described in Thomas Fuller's *History of the Worthies of England* (1662): 'Somerleyton Hall . . . well answering the name thereof: for here summer is to be seen in the depth of winter in the pleasant walks beset on both sides with fir trees green all the year long, besides other curiosities.'

My brief here was to make reference to the earlier garden without compromising the important mid-nineteenth-century one designed by W. A. Nesfield (from 1846) and Joseph Paxton (from 1851), and to simplify and make more architectural Nesfield's large west parterre. The garden had been laid out using many of the axes and much of the geometry of the older garden, so it is literally on top of the earlier layout. As is the case with many houses in the nineteenth century, it had been turned round so that the entrance front (once on the west side) was moved to the east. This was one of Repton's favourite hobby horses: the idea that it is a waste to throw away a good aspect on an entrance hall and carriage sweep. I tend to agree and have often suggested a similar change.

The replanting of the west parterre, for which Nesfield's original design survives, was led by the broad scale of the original, which had disappeared in the 1940s - with its embroidered pattern outlined in white gravel, it was thought to be too visible and identifiable from the air. Much of Nesfield's shrub planting has been used - *Phillyrea latifolia*, yew and

Somerleyton Hall, Suffolk. The lost parterre designed by W.A. Nesfield has been updated using structured evergreen planting on a bold scale. The massed planting of *Santolina incana* infills spaces defined by broad swathes of box that follow the outer perimeter of the original complicated *parterre de broderie*. The central fountain is a recent introduction.

OPPOSITE, ABOVE Somerleyton Hall, the parterre, looking towards the astrolabe which was the termination of Nesfield's design. The astrolabe has recently been regilded and this, along with the glitter of a water jet, adds animation to the design. The all-green planting relies for its effect on contrast of texture and different shades of green. The shallow stone vases originally planted with summer bedding now hold phormiums, which have year-round impact and require little water.

OPPOSITE, BELOW Somerleyton Hall. The west facade has been articulated at ground-floor level with yew balls and *Phillyrea latifolia* mopheads between the windows. Earlier plantings of climbing roses against the walls have been pruned to keep below the first string course. At the outer corners *Rhamnus alaternus* has been trained against the wall to flank the bay windows. Phillyrea, rhamnus, yew and box (all staples of seventeenth-century gardening) were part of Nesfield's original planting scheme. He had a collection of seventeenth-century designs for parterres, which formed the chief inspiration for his own schemes.

hornbeam – but the complex box parterre with coloured gravels based on seventeenth-century French prototypes has been much simplified on broadly the same footprint using *Santolina incana* and box. This replaces the rose beds that had been a post-war insertion. The whole garden is an essay in topiary and monochrome colour - grey and green - so that sculptural shapes predominate. The rather overgrown Irish yews, probably the Nesfield originals, have been retained, as they give scale and their quirky shapes make a nice contrast with the strict geometry of the layout. All the surviving stone detailing and ornament have been kept. The one insertion is a plain central round pool with a simple jet. Its stone coping is copied from one of the Portland stone raised bed edgings which flank the main parterre and are part of the original scheme.

Next to the house *Rhamnus alaternus* columns have been inserted between the windows, along with *Phillyrea latifolia* mopheads, below which are yew balls. Climbing roses, which were already there, have been kept and supplemented with new ones, but trained to reach only to the first-floor windows. The general effect now is of a structured seventeenth-century garden, using in the main plant material from that period, overlaid on the Nesfield footprint: it looks early twenty-first century but has aspects of both the seventeenth and the nineteenth centuries.

The regilding of the magnificent astrolabe on a raised grass mount at one end of the parterre adds a sense of glitter and enriches the all-green colour scheme. I am a great believer in outdoor gilding, which, if sparingly used, has a very enlivening effect, and I quite often suggest it on both garden ornament and architecture. Repton wrote: 'The colour of gold, like its material, seems to remove all difficulties, and makes everything pleasing' (*Theory and Practice*, 1803).

Next to the west parterre, the site of the huge 1850s winter garden has been given structure by the addition of large mophead Portugal laurels, which have the effect of orange trees, centred on the remaining arcaded windows of the winter garden.

AT OXNEAD HALL, a house with a strong Repton connection since his brother John was the tenant, there is a similarly layered garden, though in this case the dates are of a wider span. The house, though large, is now only a fragment, a service wing, of the even bigger one built by the Pastons from the fifteenth century onwards, the greater part of which was demolished in the 1730s. The sixteenth-century terracing, forecourt, gate lodges and footprint of the house survive, however, and

underwent an inventive and free reconstruction from the 1980s by the photographer John Hedgecoe, who also added a new wing (not on the original footprint). Following his death, new owners have taken a much less complicated and more rigorous view on the restoration of the garden. It is relatively well documented, and in fact John Adey Repton, Humphry's eldest son, published a conjectural restoration of the house and garden.

In the ongoing restoration the main points have been remaking the forecourt with its interesting surviving piers, walls and lodges, and planting the ground plan of the house in yew so that the axial progression from the forecourt through the house to the tiered garden beyond is to some extent reinstated. The central axis of the garden ran straight through the centre of the house from front door to garden entrance, and without this linking vista the transition from the plain grandeur of the forecourt to the richer complexity of the garden terraces lacked point. Some of the Hedgecoe planting has been retained in a simplified form, which gives the main parterre in particular an air of maturity and age. Several garden buildings also by Hedgecoe have been retained, even though they were almost thrown up, for theatrical effect, using modern materials.

The setting for the house has a Reptonian sense of movement from formal foreground to informal middle ground and distance. The earthworks and walls define the main formal areas, and luckily twentieth-century gates and an extraordinary late sixteenth-century triumphal arch frame views into a

Oxnead Hall, Norfolk. The parterre made by John Hedgecoe, a previous owner, has been simplified and its ornament reduced. The garden and the majority of the house were lost in the early eighteenth century but were conjecturally reconstructed by John Adey Repton in the early nineteenth. It was a house of interest to the Reptons, as Humphry Repton's brother John was the tenant in the late eighteenth and early nineteenth centuries.

An imagined reconstruction of the sixteenth-/seventeenth-century house and garden at Oxnead by John Adey Repton. Only the rear wing on the far right and the adjacent barns survive, though the footprint of the main house has recently been outlined in yew to make some sense of the surviving courtyard to the north, which is on its central axis.

transitional formal/informal area to the east, which has been recast in a style of simplified formality, giving way beyond that to informal 'dressed' woodland. To the west beyond a raised-earth viewing platform, an area intersected by lime avenues has been created on the site of the original kitchen garden (as conjectured by John Adey Repton).

One of the problems frequently encountered in historic houses of all dates is the reduction in landholdings that often happens over time, with a consequent reduction in the capacity to control views and sometimes a necessity to change the approach. At Oxnead the approach must have been a long axial one from the north, but this is now reduced to a short oblique drive that rather lowers the impact of arrival. A longer axial approach would give it one of those drop-dead first views such as you get at nearby Blickling, with one courtyard giving way to another which finally frames the spectacular house.

Repton had a discerning eye for historic architecture, and one of his many contributions to the history of taste was his enthusiasm for what he identified as 'Elizabethan Gothic' and the invention of a formal style of garden to go with it. He was perhaps one of the first garden designers to make an in-depth study of garden history and to use historic documents as a design resource. His 'Elizabethan' works include Beaudesert in Staffordshire, Barningham in Norfolk, Michelgrove in Sussex and Blickling in Norfolk. All of these places are significant in that their character has been set by the style of the building, which gave the clue to the whole look of the place.

ALBEMARLE HOUSE IN VIRGINIA is a modern building designed by David Easton in the late 1980s in an eighteenth-century American style. At the same time a large park and garden were put together with advice from François Goffinet. Because the house is set into a hillside, it has extensive views from the entrance front over a vast tract of rolling wooded countryside, the foreground and middle ground of which were thrown

Oxnead Hall. Looking from the raised-earth viewing platform towards the main parterre. The garden leads from the house to the river Bure in a series of wide terraces. The arcaded building to the right of the oak is the remains of a sixteenth-century triumphal arch that may have housed sculpture. The octagonal tower to its left was rebuilt on old footings by John Hedgecoe.

The view from the front terrace at Albemarle House, Virginia. This vast view is one of which Repton would not have approved - he thought a panoramic 'stare' does not make a picture and needs a foreground frame to render it a pictorial composition. In this instance I added flaming balls on brick plinths as well as stone bollards, both to provide a low foreground frame and to make the terrace wall feel less precipitous

into one space articulated by large groups of trees and extensive artificial lakes. Behind the house a formal garden is set into the hillside, with various terraces linked by staircases. I came to the site after much of this had matured into a landscape that Repton would have recognized as in his manner.

However, from the front it lacked what he would have considered essential: a foreground frame. He realized that a panorama, however startling, does not make a pictorial composition. To correct this I suggested some foreground planting below the raised terrace which forms the entrance forecourt, as well as some tree planting that frames the building from the approach. The front drive winds uphill for about half a mile - with the house sometimes in view and sometimes hidden. It approaches the house in a way that Repton would have approved, in that it is not axial (indeed this would not be possible in this topography) but at an angle of 45 degrees to show the three-dimensional quality of the house to better advantage. Looking out from the terrace, the addition of flame finials on new piers, as well as obelisk-shaped bollards linked by chain, give a frame to the view and throw the vast perspective into greater relief.

Against the front of the house a new massed underplanting of box topiary and Italian cypress keys the building into the landscape from a distance and presents a green foreground from close to. To the left the garages and ancillary buildings are visually separated from the main house by more evergreen planting, but still read as part of the overall mass of building from a distance, increasing, as Repton would have been pleased to note (and to use his often repeated phrase), the 'apparent extent' of the dwelling.

This assemblage by its recent owner, Patricia Kluge, is a rare instance in the late twentieth century of a large house and garden being put together on a truly eighteenth-century scale - what Repton would have called 'a creation', since there was nothing here before except an attractive farming landscape and a modest farmhouse which forms the central core of the present house: a nice Georgian touch, as many large historic houses have grown from just such a modest core.

MEDIUM-SIZED COUNTRY HOUSES

It is not by adding field to field, or by taking away hedges, or by removing roads to a distance, that the character of a villa is to be improved: it is by availing ourselves of every circumstance of interest or beauty within our reach, and by hiding such objects as cannot be viewed with pleasure. (*Fragments*, 1816)

WHILE THE LARGE HOUSES DESCRIBED ABOVE might be types recognizable by the late Georgian improver, the medium-sized country house of today would perhaps have been categorized by Repton as a villa - that is, a smaller house without a large landed estate, probably in the proximity of a town, to provide the occasional residence of perhaps a merchant, lawyer or banker, someone whose principal home is of necessity in town. This sort of house, about which Repton is slightly disparaging, is the ideal today since it can be kept up with less expense and is easier to shut up for intermittent use.

Its appurtenances, too, might be scaled down and somewhat different in style, perhaps with an emphasis on pleasure grounds - what he would have called 'dressed grounds' - close to the house. Often such houses benefit from borrowed landscape: that is, if they are set in a pleasing landscape not necessarily belonging to the house. In this case, the views from the house can be carefully framed to exclude what is unpleasant and to highlight what is good. Repton did this to perfection in his first commission on the outskirts of London at Brandsbury (see page 8), a villa with about a hundred acres now overrun by the suburb of Willesden. Today, with much quicker travel, small houses can be further from a metropolis, and in fact this lends appeal since the settings will probably be less spoiled by development or suburban sprawl.

A complete volte-face in taste has made the sort of house that Repton despised - the cubic early eighteenth-century red brick symmetrical block - today the most desired house type. He very often suggested rendering and painting old red brick houses a stone colour, on the grounds that red does not accord well with the greens of a landscape. This is a view with which most people today would disagree. But, of course, we now have the advantage of two hundred years of patination and weathering.

Repton thought that the character of a property is conveyed in the first glance and therefore first impressions are crucial. This makes the approaches, drives and outer edges of the grounds as important as the inner recesses of a garden, if not more so.

Before and after sketches by Repton for Hoveton House, Norfolk. This scheme was not carried out and the house remains much as it is shown in the upper view - a slightly naive though charming baroque composition. Repton's surviving correspondence describes other improvements that were in part implemented.

THE MANOR HOUSE, WEST STAFFORD, is a small manor house in a Dorset village, with a good deal of privacy and views across water meadows on the entrance side and across its own ground on the garden side. This early seventeenth-century house was once approached axially from the south via elegant entrance piers with baroque urns flanked by iron grills. In the early nineteenth century, just as Repton would have advised, the entrance was swapped to the north via a small oblique lane that is still the approach. At the same time, the back of the house gained a new facade to smarten it up as the entrance front.

The first change I made here was to slightly reroute and plant up the drive so that the house is not seen until it is almost reached. New planting also created a separate parking space so that cars are not seen from the entrance front of the house. Then, to give interest to what is distinctly the plainest facade, I decided to create two short canals in front of the house. They give a symbolic link to the water meadows beyond and create a reflective mirror that makes the relatively low house more imposing.

At West Stafford the garden is designed to align with the various doors and windows of the house, each facade having a different theme. On

OPPOSITE, ABOVE The Manor House, West Stafford, the north front. The entrance was changed from the south front in the early nineteenth century. The original baroque gate piers survive to the south, and the drive from that side has been recently reinstated, though leading now to the north.

OPPOSITE, BELOW The attractive mid-eighteenth-century east front of the house, framed by pleached limes, is now glimpsed from the reinstated south approach.

BELOW The twin canals make a visual link to the lovely managed water meadows below. A curve of pleached limes in the background forms an apsidal end to the enclosed lawn on the east side.

the main garden front the land slopes upwards from the house, so I have used a zigzag arrangement of narrow beds - a modern version of the *plate-bande*, or narrow linear bed of the late seventeenth century - that draws the eye upwards. A bold pattern is seen to better advantage on an upward slope where it is less foreshortened. The view beyond the canals at the front is framed by two simple blocks of fenced formal tree planting, which have the effect of carrying the vista out towards the grazed water meadows.

A completely separate walled garden houses all the functional elements of the garden: a swimming pool, tennis court and kitchen garden. These are hidden from the view of the house but are close by. Repton liked to hide kitchen gardens but make them near to stables to be able to benefit from the manure.

THE HOUSE NOW KNOWN AS MODEL FARM, HOLKHAM, was built by Samuel Wyatt in the 1780s as an inn for the Holkham estate. As it overlooks the park, it gets all the borrowed landscape you could desire. In the 1860s a model farm was built in front of it with elaborate accommodation for livestock. Lord and Lady Leicester moved to the house when Lord Leicester's son took over Holkham Hall; they radically altered it inside, while keeping the external architecture exactly as it was. As it had been used as a grain store after the Second World War, the interior was pretty well gutted.

The farm buildings form an attractive enclosed forecourt to the house, with an elegant arch, through the central barn, that makes the main entrance drive to the house. A ventilator in the form of a decorative turret announces from the road that this is the main entrance. The low piggeries that once stood in the middle of this yard were demolished many years

ABOVE The entrance courtyard at Model Farm, Holkham, Norfolk. This courtyard was originally part of the model farm buildings built in the 1860s. It has been adapted to make the arch in the west range form the main entrance drive to the house.

OPPOSITE, ABOVE The irregular massing of the house and its offices is Reptonian in feel. Repton rather approved of visually linking the house and its outbuildings to create a picturesque mass softened by strategic planting.

OPPOSITE, BELOW This conservatory was designed to link the main house with the offices and at the same time to create an everyday sitting room. Not unlike Repton's idea of the dual-purpose library/conservatory, this room is directly linked to the garden.

ago, leaving a spacious forecourt that I planted with limes and pleached hornbeams; the latter were set out to frame the front door of the house, which is not on the central axis of the yard.

Internally, the house was skilfully put back together by Nicholas Hills, and I designed a conservatory that links the main house to the service block to make a large, light sitting room - the equivalent of Repton's 'Modern Living Room' from Fragment XIII of *Fragments*: a multipurpose and relaxed space that combines sitting room, library, conservatory and general meeting area.

Elsewhere in this garden a formal canal flanked by lead-roofed pavilions is viewed from the double drawing room on the south side of the house. To the east a ha-ha creates an invisible barrier between park and garden. To the north a walled garden is separated from the main garden by old *Quercus ilex* (evergreen oak) trees, for which Holkham is famous. They are supposed to have arrived in the early eighteenth century as acorns from the packing material for Grand Tour purchases made in Italy by Thomas Coke, Earl of Leicester (1697-1759), who built Holkham.

FARMHOUSES

If the yeoman destroys his farm by making what is called a 'Ferme ornée', he will absurdly sacrifice his income to his pleasure: but the country gentleman can only ornament his place by separating the features of farm and park. (*Theory and Practice*, 1803)

THE CHARACTER OF A FARMHOUSE would have horrified Repton. In the stratified society of his day there was a wide gulf between the life of a gentleman farmer and one who is actively involved in the physical process of farming. At the same time, many landowners were well aware that their livelihood depended on it, and such agricultural reformers as Coke of Norfolk were knowledgeable and forward-thinking in their farming practice and took great interest in it.

Today the small farmhouse is an admired building type, especially where there are nearby farm buildings that can be adapted to provide additional accommodation; and while Repton's misgivings on the subject of applying inappropriate grandeur to a simple building might still apply,

BELOW The Farm, New Hampshire. This small estate is run as what might in the eighteenth century have been called a *ferme ornée*. It contains no permanent house and is occupied from an eighteenth-century town house nearby. This circular pool with its Rabbit Island was designed to set the rather fantastical tone of the site and is seen from the long entrance drive. It was inspired by the ornamental rabbit warren and island at the Valsanzibio garden near Padua, though it has been given an American dress.

it is nevertheless possible to create a formal garden not out of tune with the rustic simplicity of the architecture. The idea of the *ferme ornée* is also still current; the supposition is that a small farming operation can be made aesthetic and indeed be included as an integral part of the designed landscape. Today we go beyond the Repton ideal of a grazed park to include orchards, vegetable gardens and poultry yards into the aesthetic parts of a garden, while in his day these important functions might well be hidden behind walls or plantations. There has been a return to the seventeenth-century idea that functional elements add to the beauty of the whole ensemble.

At Silverstone Farm, my own house, a small farmhouse is set in the middle of its two-acre plot, which makes it possible to garden on all sides of the building. The detached farmyards are also taken into the scene and gardened in an architectural way. As is usually the case, they face south and are enclosed on three sides to provide a sheltered space, which lends itself to very simple formal planting of the type you might find in a university quadrangle. The central one of my three yards is laid out as four grass plats intersected by gravel walks.

BELOW The chicken garden at Friston Place. This walled enclosure near the house has been treated as an ornamental but functional enclosure for hens. The chicken run is surrounded by posts with finials of large gilded lead eggs. The other half of the garden is planted as a nuttery, with hazel, walnut and almond trees.

OVERLEAF Tilbury Hall, Suffolk, the kitchen garden. The raised beds in this walled garden are strongly inspired by the *potager* at Villandry in the Loire Valley. At the centre, oak carpenter's work niches planted with vines surround a round pool and fountain.

BELOW Silverstone Farm, Norfolk, the central courtyard. This farmyard, one of three enclosed by early nineteenth-century farm buildings, has been treated very simply with four grass plats. To the left a south-facing cattle shed has been glazed to provide winter housing for orange trees and house plants. The large gilded ball came from Sea Container House in London. The mophead trees in tubs are *Phillyrea latifolia*.

OPPOSITE, ABOVE Columbine Hall, Suffolk, the newly formed entrance arch in a range of reconfigured farm buildings. This arch forms a direct link to the bridge across the moat that is the only approach to the house. The moat encloses more than an acre of ornamental garden as well as the house itself.

OPPOSITE, BELOW The herb garden created on the edge of the moat at Columbine Hall.

An open cattle shelter has been converted into a glasshouse by glazing the south-facing open side. I think the important point in a farmyard is not to tidy it up too much, and to live with the rough and worn surfaces that farm animals and long usage generate. The mistake made with most barn conversions is to treat their surroundings as a conventional flower garden. The greatest simplicity, with an element of formality, seems to suit much better.

FARMYARDS CAN ALSO MAKE A GOOD WAY TO APPROACH A HOUSE. An interesting group of picturesque buildings can often be rearranged to build up a sense of approach, especially if a drive actually passes through them. This again would have been anathema to Repton, though he would have appreciated the general idea of creating a gradual accumulation of incidents along a drive as it approaches the house. At Columbine Hall in Suffolk I used the clapboard buildings that stand at the entrance to the medieval moated hall house to form, as it were, gate lodges to the house and its garden, which are both actually within the moat. This involved the removal of modern steel grain silos and barns to reveal the traditional timber-framed ones. By linking two of them

with a simple entrance arch and open cart sheds in the same style, I created an axial drive leading to the earth bridge that crosses the moat (see page 82). The original drive went round the outside of these barns, making a less direct route. The buildings are still put to good use; one has been converted to a cottage, another to a large events room, and the rest are used as workshops. Within this complex a walled kitchen garden has been created, as well as space for parking to hide cars from the larger landscape.

COKE OF NORFOLK, Earl of Leicester (1754–1842) was criticized by some of his contemporaries for building gentlemen's houses for his tenant farmers: the Red House is one of his elegant farmhouses. In recent years it had been separated from its extensive barns and outbuildings. The first step, therefore, was to design new stables that also form a new approach to the house through an archway into the stable yard. From mid-nineteenth-century large-scale Ordnance Survey maps - a useful resource in working out the recent

history of gardens in relation to buildings – I discovered that there had been a similarly sized building on the same site with much the same footprint.

The garden is largely on the north side of the house and on a steep downward slope, giving way to a small park-like series of fields on an upward slope. The foreground garden is terraced, and at the lower level I made a raised semicircular lawn that cuts into the informal landscape, creating a link between the formal and the informal.

One of Repton's simple but effective tricks to hide the piecemeal effect of hedgerows and field boundaries was to plant irregular clumps of trees attached to the field boundaries or positioned in their corners, to break up the straight lines and to lose the effect of paddocks. I have used just this device here to make the necessary fenced paddocks seem part of a larger informal landscape.

OPPOSITE The Red House. The new stable block, on the site of an old outbuilding which had disappeared many years ago, is built partly of oak and partly of brick and flint under a pantiled roof. It is linked to an existing building which has been turned into a lodge cottage facing the entrance drive, but forms part of a larger composition which includes the house.

LEFT The original entrance front of the Red House is south-facing and has been turned into a simple gardened forecourt. Cars are now brought to the back of the house through the new stable block. There is separate parking hidden near the entrance gate.

COTTAGES

An irregular farmhouse, little better than a cottage, backed by a hill
and beautiful group of trees, presented an object so picturesque,
that it was impossible to wish it removed and replaced by any other
style of building. (Proposals for Endsleigh in Devon for the Duke of
Bedford, 1809, quoted in Fragment XXXIV, *Fragments*, 1816)

THE *COTTAGE ORNÉ* of the late eighteenth and early nineteenth centuries
was devised to elevate an ordinary cottage into one that was very
evidently not inhabited by an agricultural labourer; it was marked out
by the addition of ornament that need not be too complicated: perhaps
a verandah, a thatched roof of picturesque outline, green shutters or
Gothic windows. Repton and his two architect sons, John Adey and
George, made quite a few essays in this style - some of them quite large
houses dressed up (or rather down) as cottages. They might be built -
or adapted - for occasional use as fishing lodges or hunting boxes, or
created as secondary houses on estates, as, for instance, Uppercross
Cottage described in Jane Austen's *Persuasion* (1815), a pre-existing house
made genteel by a new verandah and French windows.

The picturesque cottage is still a very sought-after building type,
having been given a new aesthetic interest under the guidance of the
Arts and Crafts movement and the houses and gardens of Edwin Lutyens
and Gertrude Jekyll in the late nineteenth and early twentieth centuries.
I have tried to give a rather different view of what could constitute an
appropriate style for a cottage garden, based less on the picturesque and
more on the simple formality of real cottage gardens - by which I mean
that unselfconscious, ordered mixture of utility and ornament that can
still sometimes be seen in the countryside. They were particularly well
recorded by the photographer Edwin Smith in the 1950s.

THE ENGINE HOUSE AT SILVERSTONE FARM is a converted flint and brick
barn originally built in 1864 to house a steam threshing engine. The
garden here is very simple - two hornbeam-hedged enclosures facing
east and west which frame an open central lawn flanked by cubed limes
and divided by a central gravel path. The point here is that the cottage,
on a private lane and in the middle of an agricultural landscape, should
not look too decorated, though it is given a certain distinction by being
set in a simple symmetrical layout.

Silverstone Farm, the Engine House.
This detached outbuilding designed
to house a steam thrashing machine
in 1864 has been turned into a two-
bedroom cottage. It is approached
by a short avenue of pleached limes
and through a domed hornbeam arch
trained on a timber frame.

THE GARDENER'S COTTAGE AT THENFORD is a 1930s building set into the walls of a large eighteenth-century kitchen garden. It was a plain symmetrical building with a good roof of peg tiles but had unattractive steel windows and a mean central door. We gave it timber Gothic casements set within the original openings and added a metal porch with a copper canopy. The new half-glazed door was given visual substance by adding a wide timber architrave.

CONSTANTINE COTTAGE, right on the edge of a Cornish cliff, has spectacular views, but its exposure and geology are not conducive to gardening. The outward view is the principal point of the site, and the small foreground enclosed by a low stone wall on the very brink of the cliff is the only garden. The idea was that gardening should be very low key and planted with the sort of native material that would survive the rigours of this exposed position. In such a windswept site trees struggle to survive, so planting is essentially ground-hugging and forms a very close-up foreground to the grand sweep of the bay. Anything more formal or elaborate would strike a jarring note against the grandeur of nature and the simple architecture of this former coastguard's cottage.

BELOW The Gardener's Cottage at Thenford now sits between new long ranges of south-facing glasshouses. On the right are domed pavilions that punctuate the garden, emphasizing its diagonal grid layout. (For an aerial view, see page 98.)

OPPOSITE, ABOVE Constantine Cottage, perched on a Cornish cliff, has a very small garden, partly open to the view of the bay and partly enclosed by hedges of tamarisk and griselinia planted as wind protection on raised stone banks

OPPOSITE, BELOW Simple stone steps link the open lawn to the enclosed one.

SITUATION

Character teaches what is advisable whereas
Situation tells what is possible to be done.

SKETCHES AND HINTS, 1795

I N HIS SKETCHES AND HINTS Repton proposed a list of circumstances that define a situation:

Firstly: The natural character of the surrounding country.

Secondly: The style, character and size of the house.

Thirdly: The aspects or exposure, both with regard to the sun, and the prevalent winds of the country.

Fourthly: The shape of the ground near the house.

Fifthly: The views from the several apartments.

Sixthly: The numerous objects of comfort: - such as dry soil, a supply of good water, proper space for offices . . .

He goes on to say that these refer to a mansion in the country, but some of the criteria may not apply, or may be very differently disposed, in a town garden.

Every location must be dealt with in a different way, and Repton used as illustrations widely divergent terrains to describe this diversity. In my work a wide range of locations offer very different topography, and I have chosen here deliberately contrasting sites to illustrate the fact that Repton's observations are still relevant. Even urban plots have features that situate them in their own peculiar sphere, and once this individuality has been identified it becomes easier to enhance what is good and to suppress or hide what is unattractive.

The view over a raised front garden giving on to Park Lane, London. The raised Portugal laurel
hedge is high enough above street level to hide double-decker buses, which pass within a few feet.
The canopy of trees is from Hyde Park on the other side of the road.

COUNTRY GARDENS

FRISTON PLACE is wonderfully hidden in a fold of the countryside. It is in a valley bottom and the soil is thin over limestone. The land immediately surrounding the sixteenth-century manor house was originally enclosed and subdivided into a series of geometric compartments by flint and brick walls. These walled sections formed the drive, an entrance court, a kitchen garden, doubtless an ornamental garden and other functional spaces. They must have also given a sense of security against the then bleak and remote downland setting.

In the early 1950s the garden was redesigned by the prolific Percy Cane for the present owner's parents. His contribution was to remove some of the dividing walls, which opened up longer views from some of the principal rooms - notably a long double border (see pages 110-11) that leads off the drawing room terrace newly created by Cane. Part of my contribution has been to reinstate some of these divisions, using beech hedges rather than walls, so that the pre-existing rose garden is now a separate room, with a beech hedge on its once-open fourth side.

BELOW Friston Place. The entrance gates lead to the front door, opposite which is a seventeenth-century donkey house whose internal wheel was used to raise water from the well. Flanking the door of the donkey house is a pair of lead cisterns with small fountain jets.

OPPOSITE Tiered beech hedges create a 'mount' in the centre of the rose garden.

This gives it more impact. It was once one of the principal ornamental gardens - as you can tell from its more decorated Gothic arched gate openings - and it has become again one of the richest parts of the garden, with a series of ornamental features that add interest to the box-edged rose beds.

The garden has interesting changes of level, which on the south side rise away from the house - a situation that offers scope for steps and staircases, which have been emphasized by planting. The original designers of the garden made clever use of the hillside, turning it into a series of separate level terraces, which increase the element of expectation and surprise as you move from one to the other. To the north the land descends, and at the bottom of the valley two large flint-walled enclosures house a large ornamental poultry yard and a pool garden.

HIGHAM PLACE IN SUFFOLK, a beautiful medieval - but externally Regency - house, is set in the most magical countryside. But even with long and spectacular views there needs to be a frame and diversification of the foreground to give point and direction. Here each front of the house has been given a different treatment.

The principal view to the south across a small park is the most open, allowing for long views across Dedham Vale, Constable's most painted landscape. (In fact, there is a Constable oil painting showing this house set in the middle distance of the view.) The park has been improved in the past twenty-five years with an irregular belt plantation along the road to the west hiding the traffic, and an avenue due south connecting to a new drive.

Since the land falls to the south, it has been possible to create two enclosed gardens without

Pleached limes form a cross walk between the edge of Friston's formal garden and a series of grass terraces. Beneath the limes is a wild flower meadow planted on thin soil over limestone.

hiding the view. These are different in style. The first, aligned on the drawing room, is enclosed by yew hedges and has a double row of *Pyrus salicifolia* framing a trellis pavilion. The second vista leads from the garden door towards a flint obelisk in the distance backed by an exedra (semicircular recess) of Italian cypress.

On the east side of the house, originally a service wing with a jumble of small rooms, I designed a new facade and reconfigured the rooms to create a large garden drawing room below and a large bedroom and bathroom above. These overlook two enclosed gardens - the first walled on two sides and facing a yew hedge pierced by iron gates on brick piers. This garden is planted with herbaceous borders next to the house below the new lowered sash windows. Two sphinxes on plinths flank the gate. Beyond this a very plain tapered enclosure is hedged with hornbeam, and beyond that are further enclosures gradually less formal in treatment. To the west, the entrance front of the house, which is quite close to the road, has been given an enclosed forecourt with tall yew hedges, the attractive bow-windowed stucco facade of the house providing all the interest needed. To the north, a small walled vegetable garden leads off the kitchen, with a miniature south-facing lean-to glasshouse. This leads to another enclosed garden with a south-facing grotto-like alcove at the centre (see page 199).

The problem of where to make the main approach to this house has been solved by using what was the back drive, entering at the road past a 1930s lodge cottage through existing hornbeam hedges. This low-key approach has the effect of gradually revealing the garden and house as a series of small incidents ending at the front courtyard with the impressive entrance front of the house - which is in fact also on the village street, though hidden from it by a yew hedge.

OPPOSITE, ABOVE Higham Place, Suffolk. A new occasional approach from the south is defined by an avenue of limes. New park rail fencing separates the grazed parkland from the pleasure ground.

OPPOSITE, BELOW Yew-hedged compartments are axised on the drawing room's French windows. The vista terminates in a covered seat flanked by grey *Pyrus salicifolia* standards.

ABOVE, LEFT A new facade to the east elevation. This wing, once small service rooms, now houses a large drawing room that engages with the garden on this side. The 'Gibbs' doorcase was designed to add architectural interest.

ABOVE, RIGHT A new clapboard L-shaped stable block was designed to complete a service yard and to provide storage and offices.

Mill Farm, Suffolk. The gable end elevation of the house was redesigned to make more of the view from this side of the house to the water. The glazed extension was added to bring a small sitting room closer to the sound and sight of the mill-race.

AT MILL FARM, SUFFOLK, the proximity of the old miller's house to the mill-race gives it an exciting quality that is unique to water in dynamic movement. Repton wrote about the constant sound and the glitter of light on water in many Red Books. He was particularly interested in how light falling on water or other objects in a landscape has a different effect at various times of day, and was inventive in the way he devised animation on the surface of water.

Here the mill building has gone, but the river and the mill-race together form the main focus of the garden. To make more of this I added a small glazed garden room right next to the water so that the house became more engaged with the river. A detached outbuilding converted by the late owner's mother into a library was linked to the house by a new glazed corridor. Both overlook the river.

The entrance front of the house, which is early eighteenth century (though altered a century later), looks away from the river across a beautiful stretch of countryside - a vista that has been opened up. Although the entrance drive crosses this vista, it does not form a significant break. Immediately next to the entrance front is a foreground of box-edged beds framing the front door. Cars are led beyond this to a

parking space out of sight of the drawing room and dining room, which flank the front door.

A vegetable and a fruit garden are on a raised bank above the house on the opposite side from the river. These form the principal ornamental elements, as it was felt the garden overall should be very simple so as not to detract from the river and the landscape setting.

TO THE NORTH OF THE RED HOUSE (see pages 56-7) ground steeply falls, then rises again. This made the creation of a new middle ground to the scene necessary. We created a raised semicircular lawn to provide an intermediate link between the large terrace at the level of the house and the informal landscape beyond. This new lawn, fringed by *Acer platanoides* 'Globosum' standards, creates in effect a ha-ha that hides the park rail division between grazed and mown grass. Repton felt that a scene needs a notional foreground, middle ground and distance so that the eye can read the actual space it is looking at - a pictorial device that translates well to real garden scenery.

The terrace of the Red House looks out on to a lower semicircular raised bank created to provide a middle ground between formal garden and open fields. A sunk park rail keeps grazing animals at a distance.

VILLAGE GARDENS

A very small object aptly placed near the eye, may hide an offensive object ten times as large; whilst a hedge of roses and sweet briars may hide the dirt of a road, without concealing the moving objects that animate the landscape. (Fragment XXXVI, *Fragments*, 1816)

THE LONG, THIN GARDEN OF THE SALTINGS, on the Norfolk coast, faces north and overlooks the salt marshes. It descends from the Edwardian house a few feet above tidal marsh level to the coastal walk at the end of the garden. The distant view of the marsh and sea is the whole *raison d'être* of the site, and everything else must be subordinate to it. Again following Repton's dictum that a scene, however small, is improved by having a notional foreground, middle ground and distance, I introduced here a foreground, which is in fact only a raised terrace with pots, immediately outside the sitting room windows. A very simple middle ground consists of a series of earth levels defined by simple horizontal bands of planting. These give the eye a scale and key with which to read the landscape beyond, and do not distract from the main point, which is the view of the salt marshes and its constantly changing effects of light on tidal water. This garden, though in a village, has the characteristics of a town garden in that it is cheek by jowl with its neighbours, which means that you have to try to insulate or frame the view from the house with vertical incidents quite close to the house – in this case *Quercus ilex* standards and pleached limes. These help distract the eye from straying left and right and focus attention on the wider landscape beyond the narrow strips of neighbouring gardens. Repton might not often have had to deal with this scale of problem (except at his own Hare Street garden), but his ideas about pictorial framing of views using *repoussoir* trees (flanking pairs to frame a view) are as relevant on a small scale as they are on a larger one.

The view north from The Saltings, on the North Norfolk coast.

BELOW I added a tall-ceilinged garden room, with a bow window, on the footprint of old service rooms to create a large, light room that faces south across the garden. The original reception rooms face north across the village street.

OPPOSITE, ABOVE A tiny entrance court leads off the village street. It is gardened simply, with clipped climbers, varied evergreen topiary and pleached hornbeams.

OPPOSITE, BELOW The small railed front garden is given some privacy by a pleached hornbeam stilt hedge. Gravel and topiary make a simple foreground to the village street which is the object of the view from the drawing room and dining room.

AN INWARD-LOOKING VILLAGE GARDEN, such as that at Blenheim House, Norfolk, has different problems, but is, in some respects, easier to deal with than one with a specific external view in a single direction. In this case the main garden is walled, with no particular outside views; instead it has external objects to hide. This village house might have been described by Jane Austen in *Mansfield Park* (1814) as 'the smallest habitation that could rank as genteel'. It had a small stable and coach house, a groom's room and tack room, and two modest reception rooms facing the village street. I added a new bow-ended garden sitting room on the back, facing south and overlooking the walled garden - making the house engage with the garden in a way that it did not as built *c.*1840. What the garden did have was a few good trees that gave it a sense of maturity and enclosure. It also had the corner of a much earlier moat that runs through several adjacent gardens - a piece of water that, tidied up, now makes the termination to the garden on the west side. A stone terrace and a simple box parterre are aligned on the bow window of the new room. The detailing of this garden takes its cue from the plain astylar classical house - the style of architecture which Repton called 'Modern or Grecian', and which he favoured (though he might not have approved of the red

brick). Repton wrote about this style of architecture in both *Theory and Practice* (1803) and in *Designs for the Pavilion at Brighton* (1808). He meant by 'Grecian' all classical architecture, but developed a further category of classical architecture which he classified as 'Modern'. This usually, though not always, meant a plan and elevation adapted to the British climate and consisted of an astylar elevation - without an order of columns - of very simple form. The villa at Brentry Hill in Bristol, described in *Theory and Practice*, is a good example of this.

Blenheim House has two fronts - east and north - that engage with the village street, and these are treated as iron-railed miniature courtyards, articulated by clipped evergreens and pleached hornbeams. These green up the building from the village street and give the streetscape a small foreground from inside the house. You could make a comparison here with the way Repton treated the view of the village street from his own cottage at Hare Street, Essex, where he gave the house a slightly enlarged foreground by enclosing a small green, and with strategic planting hid the less desirable aspects of the view, in his case a butcher's shop. Today we might not be so worried by a butcher's shop, but other aspects of a modern village, such as signage, street lighting and telegraph poles, impact on the view outwards and have been addressed here by simple screening and distraction.

The main vista in the walled garden looks west to the remains of an early moat, which terminates this view. An urn on its far bank is framed by a hornbeam arch. The mopheads are Portugal laurel, underplanted with box and *Hebe* 'Pewter Dome'.

TOWN GARDENS

In a garden surrounded by buildings it is not to be expected that all can be excluded by plantation only . . . architectural ornaments must be called in aid of vegetation. (*Designs for the Pavilion at Brighton*, 1808)

TOWN GARDENS ARE PRIMARILY INWARD-LOOKING, unless they are lucky enough to have an attractive outside vista to appropriate. Even at the Brighton Pavilion Repton had only a narrow oblique view of the sea, which needed careful framing to make it attractive.

However, though the early nineteenth-century house shown on the right has, like all its neighbours, only a very short front garden, which now looks on to the busy traffic of Park Lane, it benefits from the large trees of Hyde Park in the middle distance. The houses are slightly raised above street level but not high enough to hide double-decker buses. The solution here was to plant tall Portugal laurel hedges sufficiently high to blot out buses and trucks, and also provide some buffer against traffic noise. Against the hedges lead fountains create further distraction from the noise of the street. The rest of the area is restrained, relying on a pattern of inlaid paving and simple topiary to create a plain open space that makes the most of an overall depth of about 16 feet. The trees on the other side of the dual carriageway hint at the limitless space beyond, so that what is in reality a very restricted space feels grand and in scale with the rather tall Regency stuccoed buildings.

We had the idea of decorating the lower ground floor light well with engravings of trellis, which give a garden-like view from the basement windows. Trellis can be very effective in town gardens. Where it is used architecturally it can add scale and grandeur to even the smallest space. Repton considered himself something of a trellis specialist. He often designed trellis to articulate or enliven plain buildings, as well as devising free-standing trellis structures, fences and arbours. Detailed designs by both his architect sons survive to show that working drawings were supplied to the makers.

OPPOSITE, ABOVE On the ground floor of this Park Lane house, the glazed lanterns that light the rooms below are concealed by box edging punctuated by box mopheads. An inlaid floor adds interest and a lead fountain at the end of the vista helps to disguise traffic noise.

OPPOSITE BELOW The basement light well has been decorated with blown-up engravings of trellis. The upper edge of the engraving is framed by ivy in troughs. Italian cypresses in pots rise through two floors to articulate the area above.

The garden of this house in London's Little Venice is at basement level, a floor below the street. A rustic pavilion - with a concave heather roof which reflects the lead and zinc roof of the new dining room extension - provides a view-stopper.

THIS SUNK INWARD-LOOKING GARDEN IN LITTLE VENICE, LONDON, is surrounded on three sides by walls, and the tall white stuccoed house forms the fourth side (see page 130). Adopting a device much used in eighteenth-century town gardens, an architectural facade to terminate the main view, I inserted a rustic pavilion. It is set against a very tall brick wall clad in trellis and planted with roses and clematis. Inside the pavilion a convex mirror with twigwork frame appears to pierce the wall with a reflection of the garden. Four beds edged with *Ophiophogon nigrescens* can be seen in plan from the raised terrace above and from the study on the main floor.

THE PRINCIPAL VIEW FROM THIS MEWS GARDEN NEAR HYDE PARK is to a tall apartment block on the east side. The solution to this problem was to build at the end a central baroque pavilion, which draws attention to itself, away from the plain building behind. Existing cypress trees in the flanking spaces have been kept high to distract from the view, and a strong foreground has been provided in the form of a miniature amphitheatre, shown here with pots but now with busts on plinths - an idea inspired by the Villa d'Ayala at Valva near Salerno, southern Italy, where a miniature *teatro di verzura* has been furnished with busts to create the audience for a non-existent theatrical performance.

The baroque pavilion at the end of this small mews garden provides a backdrop to the garden as well as helping to disguise the block of flats behind. A miniature amphitheatre presents a lively foreground, while the middle distance consists of plain terraces with topiary in pots.

| 81

THE APPROACH

*. . . ought to be convenient, interesting, and in strict harmony with
the character and situation of the mansion to which it belongs.*

SKETCHES AND HINTS, 1795

IN REPTON'S ERA an approach was devised to make the most of the first view
of a house as well as to offer carefully framed views of the park. In a modern
context, the reduction in scale of houses and gardens makes the treatment of a front
garden with ten feet of drive equally important. The framing of an entrance, what
you see from the street and how character is given to an unprepossessing entrance
or drive are all now important considerations. In a rural context, where you are
likely have more space to play with, you might look at whether the initial approach
is downplayed in order to give greater impact to a more elaborate treatment as you
enter further into the site.

Repton thought that the first impression of a house and garden, however large
or small, was key to its overall effect, and that a bad first impression is very difficult
to forget, no matter how good later impressions may be. In larger houses with
extensive grounds, the approach can consist of a series of incidents that build up
to a spectacular culmination on arrival at the front door. Repton rather eschewed
the baroque notion of a formal axial approach through a progression of avenues,
straight drives and a series of courtyards, though he did think that, in the case of
early grand houses, such an approach might be retained at least in the close environs
of the house. More often he favoured an informal, oblique approach, arguing that a
first view from 45 degrees showed off the three-dimensional qualities of a building -
which it does, especially when the house is set in a spacious landscape park.

My views on approaches on a Reptonian scale have been tested at various places,
but one difference of opinion is that I tend to think a very discreet treatment of an
entrance from a road is to be preferred, unless a grand lodge or gates already exist.
It means that the further you get into the site, the more various incidents can build
up to create increasing surprise and delight.

At Columbine Hall in Suffolk, the causeway across the moat is treated is if it were a bridge, with a
simple timber handrail. A series of hedged enclosures lead to the entrance courtyard of the house.
The first yew enclosure hides parked cars from the house and from the approach.

ABOVE In the Red Book for Sheringham Hall, in Norfolk, Repton's 'after' sketch for the approach shows how the sea can be exposed and then hidden in a series of vignettes. Here is the first glimpse of the house.

OPPOSITE, ABOVE The entrance court to Kettle Hill is framed by a pair of pavilions originally designed as aviaries. They reinforce the fantasy nature of the house, which has an amazing long view of the sea and some of the character of a Regency *cottage orné*.

OPPOSITE, BELOW The understated approach to the garden at Wiveton, framed by deliberately simple palings and gates, is lined by small mopheads of *Quercus ilex*. The house is invisible from the village green from which it is approached.

Repton realized that one of the major delights of a long approach is the sequence of theatrical 'reveals' that can be achieved by clever manipulation of existing views and those created by artifice. This is particularly evident at Sheringham Hall, Norfolk, where the sea, not really visible from the house, is nevertheless carefully exposed and then hidden in a series of vignettes skilfully contrived along his new approach.

At two coastal gardens I designed my ambition was to ensure that the approaches are understated until you get close to the house. At Kettle Hill, a seaside garden on the north Norfolk coast, the fantastical nature of the house is only revealed once you are inside the gated forecourt and are presented with a pair of Gothic aviaries framing the house. At Wiveton, simple gates and palings give way to a short avenue of *Quercus ilex* standards before a surprise water garden is revealed.

ONLY ONE WING OF THE SEVENTEENTH-CENTURY STUNTNEY OLD HALL, near Ely, survived by the time the current owners took it on in the 1980s. Since then they have rebuilt it, returning it back to a large house with the help of photographic evidence. Like many old houses it is quite near a public road - in this case, a new road built to bypass Stuntney village. In order to

insulate the house from this noisy road we created a new drive, which made possible the construction of a planted soil bund between the house and the road. The drive now leaves the main road some way from the house, higher up the hill into which the building is set (an unusual feature in this generally flat part of the Cambridgeshire Fens). This allowed for a long drive that approaches the house from above and also makes the most of the great treat of the site - a fantastic view of Ely Cathedral across the valley of the river Ouse. As it leaves the road, the drive curves into a new plantation of mixed native hardwood with evergreen underplanting and, at the gates, clumps of *Quercus ilex*, so that the first experience is of a dark wooded space. As the drive straightens out the wood thins, and you enter a flat open brow where a fairly widely spaced avenue of limes begins; the lightness of this area is made more effective by contrast with the dark plantation that precedes it. This juxtaposition of light and dark in an approach is an experience that Repton was keen to introduce, as is the placing of wilderness against well-kept neatness. A short way along this avenue Ely Cathedral is suddenly revealed, at this stage above the rooftops of the house, only to disappear again as you descend to the first courtyard via a series of yew-edged terraces. The cathedral appears again when you reach the other side of the house.

THE LARGE HISTORIC PARK AT COMBERMERE ABBEY in Cheshire was extensively replanted in 1987. Its approach from the road is about a mile long, and the parkland had not had a considered reappraisal for some years. The handing over from one generation to the next was the impetus for this renewal, and now, thirty years later, the effects of the planting are beginning to be felt. In this period major restoration of the house and stable block has been effected, and the whole estate has a well-kept look, entirely thanks to the owners, who have devoted great energy, ingenuity and funds to this historic place.

OPPOSITE, ABOVE The new approach to Stuntney Old Hall starts at a higher level than the house, so that a distant view of Ely Cathedral can be seen hovering above it.

OPPOSITE, BELOW The drive descends past a series of grass terraces whose banks are concealed by yew hedges interspersed with *Pyrus salicifolia*.

ABOVE A sequence of three watercolours showing possible treatments for the drive at Combermere Abbey.

87

THE PALLADIANIZED SEVENTEENTH-CENTURY THORNHILL PARK, with a spectacular formal garden largely designed by the late Tommy Kyle, had a drive that arrived parallel to the entrance front and too close to it. I devised a way of leading the drive away from the house so that you get a more distant axial view of the front instead of emerging directly into a courtyard right next to the house – not far enough away to appreciate the facade and its flanking formal landscape.

The house, once the family home of Sir James Thornhill, the highly successful baroque painter, was altered by him in the 1730s and was given pedimented end bays with central Venetian windows and a large obelisk in the park. Tommy Kyle built a baroque pavilion at the south end of the axis from the kitchen end of the house, which acted as a pendant to Thornhill's obelisk at the other end. On the front opposite the entrance he built a long canal on a made-up terrace with a vast Coade stone Neptune at the end of it, thus creating a foreground to the distant landscape beyond.

The new axial approach to Thornhill Park. The drive previously arrived at right angles to the entrance front. We diverted it further from the house to create this more distant view. The gate piers and ha-ha are also new.

A SIXTEENTH-/SEVENTEENTH-CENTURY DEVON HOUSE, given an early nineteenth-century Gothic dress by architect and garden designer Jeffry Wyatville, had a rather unprepossessing front drive and very plain treatment to the front of the house. I devised a double axial approach flanked by pleached limes which framed the almost symmetrical facade of the house - playing up its slightly naive Strawberry Hill quality. The drive leaves the road via an old avenue without a view of the house, and it is only on reaching the bottom of the descent and making a 90-degree turn that you see the full effect of this house that Repton might have described as 'Abbey Gothic'; it does not fit his other category, 'Castle Gothic', as it is pinnacled and crocketed with tall (down to the ground) pointed windows. Another early nineteenth-century drive with a gate lodge winds through the park from the back of the house and has been retained as an alternative, as it has an attractive view of the park though not a good first view of the house.

This new twin approach to a Devon house was created to deal with the existing drive (which descended at a steep angle and swept past the entrance front of the house to a stable yard beyond). The new arrangement allows for a level terrace which hides the sloping drive from the house but can be accessed from it.

OCCASIONALLY THERE IS SCOPE FOR MORE THAN ONE APPROACH, even on a relatively confined site. The Red House - again quite near a small lane - has a short drive which is centred on a charming small building redesigned as a lodge. The main guest parking is hidden behind hedges just beyond the entrance wall, only a short walk from the front door. However, when I designed a new functional stable block, I realized that this gave the opportunity for an additional approach to the back door through an arch set into this U-shaped timber building. The drive, descending to this arch, gives a view of the surrounding landscape not evident from the front.

SOMETIMES A HOUSE MAY HAVE NO SATISFACTORY APPROACH, and this was the case at Tilbury Hall, Suffolk, where a short drive veered unceremoniously from a dead-end lane, launching itself diagonally right across the potential garden front of this attractive medieval house and wrecking one of its best areas for gardening. A complete rethink of how the house was to be approached was led by the new garden layout and by the need for new outbuildings and garaging linked to an existing range. These became an entrance lodge with a central arch for cars, while the courtyard within provides parking and access to the house for pedestrians

BELOW The entrance gates to the Red House focus on a small cottage which acts as an entrance lodge.

OPPOSITE, ABOVE The actual vehicle entrance to the house is through the newly built stable block, which is built of oak and has brick and flint gable ends.

OPPOSITE, BELOW The view towards the house through the vertical oak boarding and oak vents of the stable block.

via a large oak cloister planted with hornbeam. The drive from this point is of grass and is used only occasionally, to get directly to the front door in bad weather. The drive itself does not impact on the landscape, but does provide some set-piece views, the first where it crosses a long tiered cascade enclosed in tall hornbeam hedges, and the last a circular forecourt surrounded by an oak carpenter's work arcade planted with hornbeam.

The visitor is encouraged to experience the garden and approach the house on foot in much the same way that you would approach a seventeenth-century house, via a series of enclosed courtyards not intended for carriages. This probably would not have appealed to Repton, but he would have been alive to the idea that a drive should not cut up the decorative parts of a garden.

The entrance gates to the garage yard at Tilbury Hall give off a newly created circle of gravel (opposite above). The barn (opposite below) was newly built to create storage and an entrance arch. The grass drive crosses a long canal in stepped sections. Visitors are usually encouraged to park in the yard and walk to the house through an oak and hornbeam tunnel arbour. In bad weather, though, it is possible to drive right up to the house via the paved turning circle (above), which is defined by an oak arcade planted with hornbeam.

WALKS AND DRIVES

*A walk which terminates without affording a continued
line of communication is always unsatisfactory.*

SKETCHES AND HINTS, 1795

W HAT REPTON IS SAYING, in this rather stilted fashion, is that a walk must always appear to go somewhere; it must also link up a series of incidents on the way. In laying out a garden the walks and visual axes are crucial. They have to relate to the house itself and to the principal views and objects in it. Thus, in the formal way of designing which I generally employ, the starting points are primarily the doors and secondarily the windows of the house. From these outward-looking points the geometry of the garden can be constructed. Even in a rectilinear garden layout the idea of a joined-up route is important, meaning, as Repton was careful to insist, that your steps need not be retraced. It is useful to bear in mind, on even the smallest scale, Louis XIV's idea of a *Manière de montrer les jardins*, so that the sequence of events and experiences is worked out in advance rather than the result of accident.

AT CHEVENING IN KENT, which has an early eighteenth-century formal layout running on both sides of a central canal, the original plan was conceived as a series of hedge-enclosed rooms framing different ornaments, natural and artificial - maybe a mature and particularly beautiful tree, or a waterwork, or perhaps an earthwork with sculptural ornament; these were linked by straight or wiggly paths defined by hedges. Some of this was reinstated by landscape architect Elizabeth Banks in the 1980s after most of the geometry had been lost in the nineteenth century. Since 2008, I have been gradually reintroducing the idea of a series of linked outdoor rooms, using Thomas Badeslade's 1719 bird's-eye view as inspiration. Because of later changes to the planting and general layout, it has not been possible to go back to the original design, but the spirit of it has been retained where possible. A long north-south avenue of limes on the east side, not part of the original layout, has provided a useful linking axis to various new features. New large-scale urns appear to terminate each end - though these are not in fact dead ends, but mark a change

These gates from the walled garden at Kettle Hill lead past the 'dressed' water
tower to an obelisk in the distance. The trellis hides stables and service areas.

of direction in the route, only apparent when you reach the end of the avenue.

Elizabeth Banks had put back some of the long diagonal rides flanked by clipped hornbeam, and these have been useful in making a visual link between the two sides of the canal, where axes have been continued across the water. There is now a linking route down both sides of the water which takes in various old and new features, including a boathouse, an octagonal yew enclosure and a mount on the east side. On the west an old commemorative urn, a pavilion containing an agglomeration of Roman inscribed tablets and a new obelisk form the focal points. It is planned to introduce more and to restore some of the once elaborate system of waterworks (see page 133). At the same time, the planting of the surrounding informal areas, which form the blocks in between the formal walks, is being intensified.

TILBURY HALL IN SUFFOLK has a largely formal garden, the various parts of which are linked by straight paths and vistas. There are, however, informal areas where winding paths follow the line of medieval fishponds and weave in and out of irregularly scattered trees (right). So there is a contrast of wildness against strict formality, which always provides an attractive counterpoint. The route round the garden should combine varied experiences, such as light areas leading to dark, open to closed, or complicated to simple. Even the smallest garden can achieve this sense of a walk through areas of varied character, and in towns one of the charms of terraced house gardens is the accidental variety that neighbouring gardens often display when viewed from upper rooms. The concept of 'variety' was in fact one of the major aesthetic tenets of late eighteenth-century picturesque theory and one Repton very often referred to and applied to the landscapes and pleasure grounds he created. He disagreed with the

picturesque theoreticians, however, about the value of studying painting for sources of variety, noting that – though painting had much else to teach – 'there was a sameness in their compositions, and even their trees are all of one general kind, while the variety of nature's productions is endless' (*Sketches and Hints*, 1795).

OPPOSITE A recently built obelisk provides a view-stopper for one of the many hornbeam *allées* at Chevening. It is sited on rising ground.

ABOVE The route around the lake garden at Tilbury Hall crosses the water channels via two bridges, one of timber, the other of tufa-clad masonry. They give two opportunities to view the waterside planting at close quarters. Nearby, timber decks jut into the lake to provide seating above the water.

RIGHT This rustic thatched pavilion with barked columns was built in a newly planted wood at Tilbury Hall, to give a focal point to the walk through it. The pavilion houses a wooden sculpture of deer, and the roof has a finial made up of antlers.

ABOVE This aerial view of the walled garden at Thenford shows how the rectilinear layout of the main paths was subdivided by diagonal ones. These made it possible to deal with the substantial slope across the garden and to make level pools in the southern quadrants: the falls being taken up in surrounding grass plats.

OPPOSITE, ABOVE The cascade is made up of a series of linked pools. These are flanked by large yew pyramids, and at the far end the composition is terminated by a shallow semicircular pool backed by a yew exedra.

OPPOSITE, BELOW The long herbaceous border on the south side of the walled garden is punctuated by Kentian seats under oak pavilions. They form resting places at intervals and face circular viewing holes in the beech hedge that encloses the other side of this long walk.

THE GARDEN AT THENFORD created by Michael and Anne Heseltine, with advice from various designers, has a number of separate formal gardens set in an informal landscape that insulates them from each other and incorporates linking paths. It is a garden with a long route on the scale of eighteenth-century parks. One emerges from woodland to find an outdoor sculpture gallery of apsidal hornbeam hedges terminating in an earth mound (designed by Robert Adams). Parallel to this is a long cascade of linked oblong pools with water jets. I designed this to fall into the first of a series of linked informal lakes underneath a new stone bridge. The bridge leads to a newly designed eighteenth-century walled garden with a walk along two of its outer sides. The formality of these areas is in contrast to an informal walk through woods, which leads to a further series of lakes in the bottom of the valley; another route takes you back to the house via a pool garden with a pavilion by Quinlan Terry, past an informal shrubbery and finally to a sunken rose garden close to the house.

THE FORMAL METHOD allows for a greater range of surface treatments of walks and drives. The ubiquitous gravel or dressed stone paving,

or pebble inlay of paths of the Repton era, is now extended by many and varied materials - often enlivened by vernacular surfaces from a variety of countries and topographies.

IN THE GARDEN OF LOS MORITOS in Trujillo, south-western Spain, hard surfaces and block plantings have replaced lawn, which would need an inordinate amount of water to keep it looking healthy. Here the paths are in fact the spaces between the grids of planted beds, and they have been laid out in a combination of cut stone and pebble work in the elaborate patterns of southern Europe. In this rocky, irregular landscape the route round the garden is, like every other element of the design, determined by the outcrops of rock that define the site, and the existing fortified walls that form the break between the garden and its magnificent distant views. The battlements still retain an elevated walkway hidden behind them, once defensive but now for viewing. This is a landscape where the foreground is the small garden space defined by the town wall, the middle ground is formed by the larger trees that have managed to survive in this inhospitable hilltop, and the distance is the endless view across the Extremadura plain towards Portugal.

AT SILVERSTONE FARM the route around the garden is defined not by paths but by openings in hedges and the distant objects framed by them. Your walk

is guided by mown vistas and view-stoppers that mark a change of direction, rather than by paths with a defined hard surface. This means that there must always be some goal to aim for, or a tantalizing glimpse of something else beyond to draw you in the right direction. I like the idea of a series of evocative inscriptions in gardens to be discovered along the route. This is an eighteenth-century idea perfected at places like The Leasowes in Shropshire, where messages relating to the various views were attached to seats. At Little Sparta in Scotland, Ian Hamilton Findlay was the modern master of the idea, where a simple landscape is enlivened by a series of incidents in the form of enigmatic inscriptions that set the tone for each separate area. At Silverstone

Farm I like to do this in a very discreet way with messages that you might or might not see. Not quite in the way that William Mason described the flower garden he designed at Nuneham in Oxfordshire in 1772, full of messages in the form of 'bowers, statues, inscriptions, busts, temples', but certainly with a series of texts, objects and buildings that allude to ideas beyond the garden.

OPPOSITE At Los Moritos beds of drought-resistant planting are defined by a grid of paths.

BELOW In this area of the garden at Silverstone Farm gravel paths are edged by box and emphasized by a series of evergreen mopheads in *Phillyrea latifolia*, Portugal laurel and holm oak.

THE FLOWER GARDEN

*Flower-gardens on a small scale may, with propriety, be formal
and artificial; but in all cases they require neatness and attention.
A flower-garden should be an object detached and distinct from
the general scenery of the place.*

THEORY AND PRACTICE, 1803

R EPTON ALLOWED FOR FLOWER GARDENS – as distinct from the more informal
planting of a pleasure ground – in the foreground of his larger landscapes. His
later work moved more towards formal flower gardens, which gave more scope
for variety in planting, ornament and layout than the informal pleasure grounds
characteristic of his earlier work.

He also had interesting ideas on colour theory. He employed the painter's device
of using only warm colours, which visually jump forwards, in the foreground of
his watercolours, gradually tailing off to bluer and greyer tones in the distance, to
imitate the effect of aerial perspective. I believe he also made use of this idea of a
warm foregound contrasted against a cool distance in actual landscapes. The colour
of flowering shrubbery in his painted views is invariably red, with the tones of the
foreground foliage warmed up with sepia pen. His aquatint 'Sunshine after Rain'
in *Fragments* (1816) illustrates the peculiar richness of colour one gets in a garden
after a rain shower, when the particles of dust through which one normally views
nature are temporarily removed. In fact, he was interested in the whole question of
how light falls on natural and artificial objects – planting, architecture and water –
devising ways to exploit the phenomena he had noticed.

IN THE 275-FOOT-LONG DOUBLE MIXED BORDERS AT PENSHURST PLACE IN KENT,
which I redesigned in 2010, I used Repton's ideas on aerial perspective to increase
the effect of such a long stretch of flowers. Partly to reduce the maintenance and
partly to create a break between sections, the long beds are broken up by lawn. Each
section has a different predominant colour scheme, and is flanked by box cubes that
form full stops between the bays. The border nearest the house is planted in shades

'Sunshine after Rain', an aquatint from *Fragments* (1816), illustrates the refreshing effect of rain on the
colours of flowers and fruit. This probably shows a scene in Repton's own garden at Hare Street.

of red, followed by orange, yellow, purple and finally blue: each colour section is 30 feet long. This idea takes up Gertrude Jekyll's notion of colour-themed mixed borders. The beds follow the line of a drive already in existence when Kip and Knyff illustrated the garden in 1719 (see page 20). They have been regularly redesigned since *c*.1900, when their first appearance as borders was photographed showing flowery underplanting to a double row of spreading apple trees. Apples have been part of the scheme ever since. In this latest version we have planted new rows of historic apples at the back of the beds - pruned as short standards to keep them from shading the planting in front of them. The old yew hedges behind the beds on both sides give a useful plain dark green background that sets the colours off well.

The overall layout at Penshurst is remarkably similar in broad outline to the compartmented plan shown in 1719. This structure gave the present owner's father the scope to introduce new detailed planting within the old framework when he restored the garden after the Second World War, and the present Lord and Lady De L'Isle have made clever changes and improvements since then, renewing planting that has become overgrown or past its best. Gardens like Penshurst that are open throughout a long season need to have an extended flowering period, and part of the planning has been to ensure that there is interest from March to October. Because it has such a good underlying architectural structure of yew hedges and walls, as well as topiary and pleached limes, the garden remains interesting throughout the year.

The long double mixed borders at Penshurst as redesigned in 2010. They were often illustrated in the early twentieth century and since then have always been backed by apples. They have now been divided into five bays interspersed by breaks of grass with box cubes, each bay in a different colour scheme, starting with red near the house and finishing in blue.

GREY AND SILVER PLANTING

I AM VERY KEEN ON GREY AND SILVER PLANTING, an idea most effectively promoted in Britain by Mrs Desmond Underwood in her 1971 book on the subject, *Grey and Silver Plants*. It was also of interest to earlier gardeners, much written about by Gertrude Jekyll, and taken up later by Norah Lindsay and Lanning Roper. From my point of view, the elimination of colour means the form and texture of plants are highlighted. I think this aspect would have been particularly appealing to Repton, given his prejudice against strong colour in the wider landscape.

Most of the plants in the grey spectrum are not native to Britain, tending to come from hotter and drier climates, but given sun and a well-drained soil they work well and look good here. They are especially successful, however, in Mediterranean climates, and I have used grey and silver plantings in France and Spain, where they thrive with a minimum of water. Block plantings of grey phormium have been used at Los Moritos in Trujillo, and in the Luberon large blocks of *Festuca glauca*, *Teucrium fruticans*, grey-leaved iris, rue and santolina are effective for most of the summer.

In the garden I designed for Christie's at the Chelsea Flower Show in 1999, 'A Sculpture Garden', the foreground planting was grey and silver - again so as not to distract with colour from the sculptural theme of the garden, which was devised to show off different works in a confined space without looking overcrowded or overly ornamented. The planting here included silver thyme, *Teucrium fruticans*, *Tanacetum densum*, *Ruta graveolens*, *Festuca glauca*, *Lavendula* 'Hidcote', *Stachys lanata* and *Helichrysum angustifolium*. The idea of these beds was to provide a loose informal foreground to a strictly structured background without distracting too much from the main subject of the garden, which was the creation of a series of framed settings for various sculptures in a variety of materials.

In my own garden (see page 178) I use pots of grey foliage subjects ranged on staging to make a bank of silver against the flint walls of the barns. The plants include *Teucrium fruticans*, *Helichrysum italicum*, *Thymus* 'Silver Posy', *Helichrysum petiolatum*, rosemary, catmint and *Hebe* 'Pewter Dome'. The clay pots have been painted in various shades of white and grey, rather than left as terracotta.

OPPOSITE, ABOVE My garden sponsored by Christie's at the 1999 Chelsea Flower Show. Because the garden was designed to showcase sculpture, the planting was predominantly monochrome.

OPPOSITE, BELOW A temporary installation at Gainsborough's House, Sudbury, to celebrate the painter's bicentenary. The architectural assemblage was designed to form a view-stopper to a primarily grey border.

MIXED BORDERS

THE MIXED BORDER - a combination of shrubs and herbaceous perennials - is in fact a Regency idea, one that has been much used in varying ways ever since. I have adapted existing borders (as at Friston Place), associated them with kitchen gardens (as at Tilbury and the Red House) and created entirely new ones (as at Oxnead).

AT FRISTON PLACE there was already a long double border, probably originally designed by Percy Cane in the 1950s. Here I built a pair of large flint obelisks sitting on clipped ivy plinths, to provide a frame and to counteract the slope in the ground that makes one border considerably higher. I also introduced periodic structural elements and clipped evergreens, to give pace. In addition, a cross vista was opened up halfway along the length, allowing glimpses of planting in the areas behind the borders. As a termination two large ivy-covered iron obelisks flank the heavily planted iron-domed temple at the centre, which is given greater presence by being smothered in clematis and honeysuckle.

OPPOSITE Opposite a new long south-facing border overlooking the parterre at Oxnead is a deliberately unruly mass of grey, white and blue designed to contrast with the ordered all-green parterre.

BELOW The long border in the walled garden at Tilbury Hall forms a backdrop to the functional raised vegetable beds inspired by Villandry.

OVERLEAF The double mixed border at Friston Place has been rearranged and augmented with foreground flint obelisks on ivy bases. A cross axis halfway along was introduced to diversify the route around the garden.

MIXING VEGETABLES AND FLOWERS, as in cottage gardens, often works well, since there is usually a formal aspect to growing vegetables. At Friston Place the vegetable garden is edged into compartments, rather like a simple knot garden. Six beds are used for vegetables and herbs; the central two have obelisk-shaped lead fountains. At the Red House the raised vegetable beds are given a central axis emphasized by a tunnel arbour.

In the walled garden at Tilbury the vegetable beds are backed by a long raised mixed border against the wall. The raised beds have at their centre trellis niches planted with honeysuckle and scented climbers. The adjacent architectural fruit cage is flanked by roses trained on iron arches.

Often flowers can enrich formal gardens without being separated off to a specific area. One use of them is in *plates-bandes*, long, thin beds in which individual flowers are strung out like jewels, popular in the seventeenth century and revived in the nineteenth century by W. A. Nesfield.

At Columbine Hall, the loose formality of the garden within the moat is enlivened by borders integrated into its green architecture, often with a seasonal aspect – so that the lime walk centred on the drawing room window is underplanted for spring interest; the emphasis moves to another part of the garden in summer.

OPPOSITE, ABOVE The kitchen garden at Friston was formed out of part of a walled paddock. The potting shed hides a glasshouse. The box-edged vegetable beds are productive, and the lead obelisk fountains in the central beds, together with the beech columns at either end, add vertical all-year-round interest.

OPPOSITE, BELOW The raised vegetable beds at the Red House have a reused old iron tunnel, planted with roses, clematis and sweet peas, running down the central path. This gives height and colour to an essentially flat display of produce.

ABOVE A vista axised on the drawing room window at Columbine Hall is defined by a lime walk punctuated by small beds. In winter the foreground hornbeam hedges and an avenue of trellis obelisks remain to focus the eye on the view across the moat.

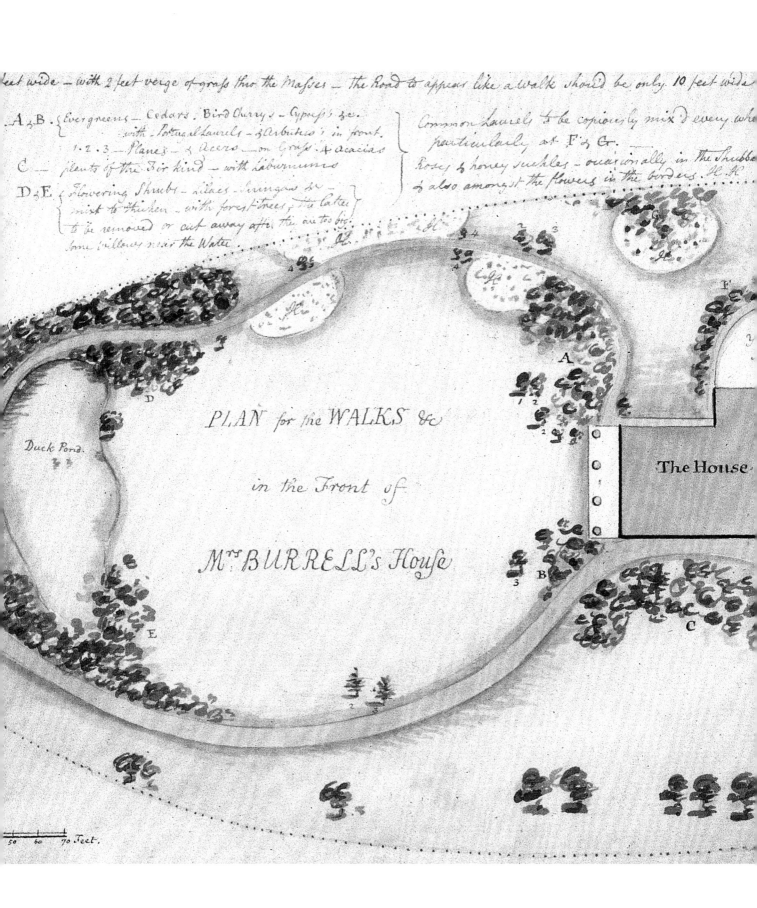

...eet wide — with 2 feet verge of grass thro the Masses — the Road to appear like a Walk should be only 10 feet wide

A & B {Evergreens — Cedars. Bird Cherrys — Cypress's &c.
       with — Portugal Laurels — & Arbutus's in front.
       1.2.3 — Planes — & Acers — on Grass. & Acacias
C —   plents of the Fir kind — with Laburnums
D & E {Flowering Shrubs — Lilacs — Syringas &c —
       mixt to thicken — with forest trees; the Latter
       to be removed or cut away after they are too big.
       Some Willows near the Water

Common Laurels to be copiously mix'd every where
particularly at F & G. —
Roses & honey suckles — occasionally in the Shrubberies
& also amongst the flowers in the borders. H.H.

PLAN for the WALKS &c

in the Front of

Mr BURRELL's House

Duck Pond

A

D

E

B

C

F

The House

50   60   70 feet.

THE PLEASURE GARDEN

This line of separation [fencing against grazing animals] being admitted,
advantage may easily be taken to ornament the lawn with flowers and
shrubs, and to attach to the mansion that scene of 'embellished neatness'
usually called a pleasure-ground.

THEORY AND PRACTICE, 1803

WHAT REPTON CALLED THE PLEASURE GROUND we might call the shrubbery and, divorced from a great estate, this type of planting eventually became perhaps the most commonly used for villa and larger town gardens. In the nineteenth century an informal lawn with paths leading through flowering shrubs and ornamental trees was the ubiquitous middle-ground scene, forming the transition between a more formal foreground and a distant landscape. It carried on through the twentieth century via exponents like Percy Cane. From the 1920s it was thought to form the most suitable setting for modernist architecture. It had the added advantage of requiring relatively low maintenance and lacked, to the uninitiated, any reference to 'period' style.

I have used this form in the way Repton did: both as a useful transitional space and as a buffer between two areas of formality of different character. To me it can be likened to a palette cleanser between two rich courses - a neutral area that makes a useful contrast and provides a visual rest. In my own garden the insulating woodland between the road and the formal areas has been partly treated in this way. Much has been written on this form of informal naturalistic gardening from Repton to William Robinson's *The Wild Garden* (1870) and Gertrude Jekyll's *Wood and Garden* (1899), with later contributions such as Christopher Tunnard's insightful *Gardens in the Modern Landscape* (1938), which documented the important role the early nineteenth century had in formulating modernist taste in landscape.

LEFT This 1790 design for the ground adjoining Mrs Burrell's house at Langley Park in Buckinghamshire is a rare example of a detailed plan by Repton for a modest-sized pleasure ground. Six-foot-wide paths wind through 'masses' of flowering and evergreen shrubbery.
OVERLEAF The pleasure ground at Tilbury Hall, in this case an informal walk through lakeside planting, makes a contrast and frame for the formal garden near the house.

WATER IN THE GARDEN

There being no part of my profession so captivating in its effect, and oftentimes so readily executed, as making a large piece of artificial water . . .

SKETCHES AND HINTS, 1795

REPTON HAD MUCH TO SAY ON THE SUBJECT OF WATER, both in the Red Books and in the published works. He was mostly interested in its informal disposition and in the animation that water in movement can add to a scene. At Ston Easton Park in Somerset he proposed the creation, from a small stream, of a wider, fast-moving shallow river, near enough to the house to add animating glitter to the gloomy north side. Water also had to look as if nature could have placed it where it was - informal water in an impossible position, such as on a hilltop or halfway down a slope, was to be avoided. On the other hand, at several sites he created slightly implausible-looking but romantic cascades and waterfalls, as at Endsleigh in Devon and Beaudesert in Staffordshire, both late works. He also took on Capability Brown's idea of making a long lake look like an imposing river by hiding its ends. In other places - as at Valleyfield, Scotland, with its canal, and Ashridge in Hertfordshire with its Gothic conduit fountain - he created formal water features. The effect of light on water was one of his major obsessions, one of the ways a static landscape could be enlivened by sparkle. The very different appearance of water at different times of day was also interesting to him: for example, a stretch of the Thames at Purley looked quite different in morning and evening, as he noted in *Theory and Practice* (1803).

One resource not available in the eighteenth century, the electric pump, has made waterworks infinitely easier to engineer. It has made it possible for me to produce the effect of water in movement, as well as apparently static reflecting pools, at several sites.

THE GARDEN OF SURPRISES at Burghley House is, of all the gardens I have designed, the one with the most elaborate water effects. Here water is the leading element and main inspiration. The sixteenth- and seventeenth-century garden at Theobalds, on which the Garden of Surprises was based, employed water in a sophisticated

'The Conduit at Ashridge', an aquatint from *Fragments* (1816), with a view of the Rose Garden and its fountain (left) and the Monks' Garden (right).

way in many fountains, grottoes and canals, and had fashionable *giocchi d'aqua*, or water jokes. The great advantage of Theobalds as a source of inspiration was that it was well described by contemporaries but had completely disappeared by the 1650s, with hardly any surviving visual evidence. This gave a much freer rein to imagining it, unhampered by very clear evidence of its appearance, but with the stimulating, enigmatic, and sometimes contradictory, descriptions of various contemporary visitors, such as Paul Hentzer in 1598, Baron Waldstein in 1600 and a parliamentary survey of 1650. Hentzner wrote: 'One goes into the garden encompassed with water large enough for one to have the pleasure of going in a boat and rowing between the shrubs.'

Gardens in this period (1565-1640) were often seen as grounds to display scientific experiment and recondite symbolism against a background of rollicking humour, which made us think of this one in a similar light; in contrast to today's gardens where horticulture is king, it foregrounds the movement of water, humour and the delights of texture and patina.

The horticultural elements are the hedges and block plantings that form a simple green framework, making rooms that separate the individual watery and other effects that are the surprises of the garden. The plant material consists primarily of hornbeam, yew, Portugal laurel, juniper, moss and ferns. You enter and exit the site through a single architectural portal of hornbeam encased by metal trellis, with the Burghley crest, a sheaf of corn, at the centre of the iron gate. The overthrow of the gate - a cluster of obelisks - is taken from an adjacent stone gateway.

LEFT The central rill at the Garden of Surprises links the Water House with a tunnel grotto of tufa. The shallow water in the rill runs over differently textured surfaces to add sparkle.

RIGHT One of the randomly intermittent water curtains in the Garden of Surprises.

ABOVE AND RIGHT Tufa arches made mysterious by a constant fog from a misting machine form an entrance to the domed Moss House. The Moss House, also of tufa, is irrigated so that its rough surface provides an acceptable home for mosses and ferns. Inside the house a viewing balcony looks into a deep misty pool and an interior studded with glittering ores, spars and crystals.

The garden is dominated by a series of random water jets and by a spinal rill that links the Water House at the higher end with a grotto at the lower. The Water House is a lead-lined pavilion in which all the interior apparatus of a house is represented in water, so that you view the room through a water curtain, behind which is a table of water, and watery 'light' in the form of a chandelier and wall sconces that emit jets. From this building a rill of water falls over an alternating pebbled and smooth surface, eventually entering a tunnel grotto of tufa framing a seated Neptune. Elsewhere in the garden are intermittent water curtains framed by door-cases surrounding a column of water which, operated by three hand pumps, raises a gold ball floating on top of it. As it reaches the top the ball triggers random jets out of the ground nearby. You have to exit the garden through a pair of tufa columns between which a 'gate' of water jets seems to bar the way, but in fact is deactivated as you approach.

In another part of the garden busts of Roman emperors, arranged in a circle, look out of windows set in a trellis screen and rotate slightly on their socles as if watching the visitor. They face inwards towards a very accurate and complex sundial, which tells much more than the local time. Elsewhere twelve more bas-reliefs of emperors stand above bubbling ponds on both sides of the rill. Finally, in an attempt to interpret the Moss House described at Theobalds, a small domed building of tufa houses a deep pool obscured by a misting machine. It is externally irrigated so that it provides a piece of rustic architecture entirely covered in moss and ferns that happily grow on the pitted volcanic rock. The Moss House is approached through a tufa arch with more mist – giving it a slightly magical and unreal setting which echoes the rather awed reports of the effects at Theobalds recorded by sixteenth- and seventeenth-century tourists.

THE MANOR HOUSE, WEST STAFFORD presents a marked contrast to the mostly moving water at the Garden of Surprises. Here the two reflective pools directly in front of the house are apparently static, designed to reflect the facade at a distance and to

LEFT At the Manor House, West Stafford, the canals have their reflective quality improved by a black lining and added black dye. They are built into a new raised terrace which acts like a ha-ha, visually separating this formal area from the more informal lawn beyond.

make reference to the managed water meadows below. Their lining is black, a colour that improves the reflective quality of the water. Between these short canals is a straight path to the front door, giving an effect rather like crossing a moat.

AT FRISTON PLACE, the pumping house still contains its water-wheel. Outside, lead cisterns form small fountains with water jets emitting from gold balls. Elsewhere in the garden Olga Polizzi has inventively re-used a pair of gargoyles that have been housed in beech columns: they spew water into tanks below. In the kitchen garden a pair of lead frostwork obelisks creates a watery centrepiece to the vegetable beds. The water clings to the frostwork faces of the obelisks, adding animation.

The pumping house at Friston Place once supplied all the water for the house, via a donkey-powered water-wheel. A pair of lead cisterns with ball fountains now recall its original function.

WATER IN THE GARDEN

At Guist Hall, Norfolk, two yew-hedged outdoor rooms already existed – one housing a swimming pool and the other, on the opposite side of a central yew *allée*, waiting to be enriched. Here we made a simple rill garden divided by gravel paths and plain grass plats. The narrow thread of water runs over long pebbles set at right angles to the flow, interspersed with riven slate, to give intermittent glitter. The water source flows through a spout below a lead Vanbrugh ball. It terminates in a transverse canal at the lower end of the garden, and at the centre is an oblong pool out of which rises an urn with four spouts. The idea is to imitate the minimal combination of grass, gravel and water found in some of the simpler treatments by André Le Nôtre, Louis XIV's gardener. At Versailles they occupy the open spaces within *bosquets*; the mature trees around this site help with the illusion that this is an outdoor room carved out of woodland.

The rill garden at Guist Hall adds the animation of water to a yew-enclosed compartment.

OPPOSITE, ABOVE In the centre of the kitchen garden at Tilbury Hall the marble fountain basin spills out into a circular bowl below.

OPPOSITE, BELOW The swimming pool garden at Tilbury, with its baroque urns.

OVERLEAF This long cascade framed by tall hornbeam hedges takes its inspiration from seventeenth-century water features, but has a simplicity of detail that puts it firmly in the twenty-first century. The pavilion at its head is a pared-down version of a Dutch garden pavilion, with gilded carved doors from south-east Asia.

AT TILBURY HALL water is one of the main themes. Here the central spinal axis of the site is a wide and long black-lined cascade, in several tiers, enclosed on both sides by tall hornbeam hedges. At the upper end a pavilion backed by trees forms a view-stopper, below which is the apparent source of the water. Its Dutch appearance is inspired by the carved wooden doors which the owners acquired from a former Dutch colony, Batavia. The lower end terminates in a croquet lawn in front of the house, a view that is framed by a pair of massive Coade stone urns. As already mentioned, the entrance drive crosses the cascade about two-thirds of the way down, giving the visitor a surprise view. Further along this drive and close to the entrance is a circular reflecting pool (see page 93), and below the entrance terrace is a string of ancient fishponds that have been incorporated into the garden route by a linked series of walks, bridges and decked landings (see pages 97, 116–117). Their margins were planted to make an interesting view from the kitchen, whose newly inserted windows are designed to overlook this attractive feature formerly not visible from the house.

The swimming pool garden here is treated as an ornamental canal rather than as a conventional pool. Rising out of it on its central axis are two specially designed baroque urns that run with water so they glisten in the sun. The tiles that line the pool, found by the owner in the Far East, are a slightly iridescent green-blue and have the surprising effect of making the water take on the changing colour of the sky.

In the walled kitchen garden there are two more water effects: an Islamic fountain with a cusped basin falls into a pool, to create the sound of running water at the centre of the garden; and on the central axis of the camellia house at the end there is a small fountain below a large Buddha's foot sculpture on the wall.

This garden has a wide spectrum of cultural references, classical and eastern, that might have appealed to Repton's sense of the exotic. He was, after all, one of the pioneers of what he called 'Hindoo' architecture and garden design in Britain, as well as being a late devotee of the taste for chinoiserie. He shared with the Prince Regent a penchant for mixing cultural and historical references, which gave a sense of fun and inventiveness to the creative life of his day.

THIS GARDEN IN LITTLE VENICE has the great advantage of being on two distinct levels: the garden at the entrance, at street level, is a floor above the lower main garden. This offers a bird's-eye view of the main garden from the entrance and made it possible to create a small cascade running between the two levels. The water is arranged primarily to be seen from the lower garden; it is hidden from the entrance at the upper level by densely planted banks. A spout at one of the upper paths flows into two levels of slate-lined runnels and then into a basin with flint retaining walls. The sound of water is especially useful in cities to help mask traffic noise, and it is valuable even here in what is, because of the heavily planted bank between the lower garden and the road, already an exceptionally quiet garden for central London.

EVEN THE SMALLEST CITY SPACE can benefit from water, as shown in a tiny Mayfair garden enclosed by high buildings. The twin rills I created were designed to be viewed from the drawing room one floor above. There is a balcony at drawing room level linked to an iron staircase that leads to the lower level, crossing the right-hand rill. The rills have small bubble jets along their length, again providing a little water turbulence

BELOW AND OPPOSITE This central London garden is unusual in offering the opportunity for a cascade. Water emits from a spout housed in a flint column at street level and runs down a slate channel to a semicircular pool at the lower main garden level. The vista is flanked by Italian cypresses which can be seen from the tent-roofed dining room that I designed as an addition to the basement kitchen.

that helps counteract the noise of the city. They are black-lined so that they reflect light and the sky into the rather shaded garden. The advantage of two narrow rills of water, rather than a single canal, in this confined area is that they visually lengthen the garden while taking up less usable space.

AT CHEVENING the site of the house would have been chosen originally for its plentiful supply of clear water direct from the North Downs. The 1719 Badeslade engraving of the garden mentioned earlier shows a series of waterworks on the east side of the canal, which must have been run from its overflow. Recently a rockwork cascade and circular pool have been reinstated roughly in the position of the one shown in the print. It is designed to have its own hornbeam-hedged enclosure, making it - like other incidents in the garden - a surprise to be discovered on a walk round the canal.

OPPOSITE Twin rills in a garden in Mayfair, London, add movement and light to a deep and dark garden at basement level. The painted walls and light-coloured gravel also help to reflect light.

BELOW This cascade and pool fed by the canal at Chevening is a recent reconstruction based on Badeslade's early eighteenth-century engraving of the garden. The original was one of a series of watery incidents that enlivened the simple formal garden. Like its predecessor, the assembly will ultimately be contained within a hornbeam 'green room', which will give it both an element of surprise and an architectural context.

LIGHT AND SHADE

I draw this conclusion: that certain objects appear best with the sun behind them, and others with the sun full upon them; and it is rather singular, that to the former belong all 'natural' objects, such as wood, trees, lawn, water, and distant mountains; while to the latter belong all 'artificial' objects, such as houses, bridges, roads, boats, arable fields, and distant towns or villages.

THEORY AND PRACTICE, 1803

THE PLAY OF LIGHT AGAINST DARK, the modelling that shadow brings to form, and the effect of light on water were all issues to which Repton devoted attention. He had, of course, only limited access to artificial lighting in gardens, but he was very alive to the effect of daylight on natural and artificial objects. His ideas are very adaptable to the modern use of electric lighting in gardens, and I have profited by his thoughts on, for instance, the direction from which objects are lit and the flattering or unflattering effects that certain orientations or different times of day can bring.

Repton wrote of the effect of back-lighting on a thin plantation - particularly on a hilltop, where the light tends to silhouette tree trunks, making a plantation look insubstantial unless it is densely underplanted. He also noted the indisputable fact that side lighting emphasizes form, whereas direct front lighting tends to flatten out objects. The quality of light at morning and evening was also treated: the warm glow of low sun, for instance, enriches colour, which is why photographers today usually prefer to work early or late in the day.

Because I generally use colour sparingly, I have been especially aware of the importance of the contrast of light and dark in planting and the uses of shadow in modelling form. Low shadows across grass can be particularly alluring, as they can increase the effect of distance and perspective, while showing up the texture of the surface.

This opening in a beech hedge at Thenford is opposite a covered seat and is designed to give a controlled view of the landscape beyond. It is trained around an iron frame. The dark frame of beech throws the light landscape beyond into greater relief. Repton used a similar device in framing a distant view with dark *repoussoir* trees.

Town gardens are often dark and overshadowed by buildings. In a garden designed for the 1999 Chelsea Flower Show I used the reflective surface of galvanized steel to bring light into the space. Broken by grey trellis, this material is too distressed to give a direct reflection, but it does have the dual effect of dissolving the boundary and reflecting light. The same effect has been used elsewhere with distressed mirror glass, sometimes in small panes, so that again only a broken reflection is present: too sharp a reflected image outdoors tends to be startling and distracting. This garden also included water with a black liner as a reflective medium. It is set against light surfaces, with dark yew topiary contrasting with grass and all seen through the lighter silver-grey foreground planting.

The Garden of Surprises at Burghley, though mainly intended for daylight visits, has artificial lighting in the form of a continuous LED strip below the the coping of the rill, forming a lit corridor the length of the site. Flanking this axis, the bas-reliefs of emperors are lit by submersible lights housed in the bubbling pools below each portrait. The ripple of the water gives movement to the lighting.

LEFT This dark-lined still canal in a garden designed for the 1999 Chelsea Flower Show is flanked by similar but narrower rills. They are devised to reflect the lit sculptures housed in the niches which form their termination. The flanking heads of Orpheus and Apollo are by Olivia Musgrave and the central Caledonian Boar by Neil Simmonds.

RIGHT A rill of water running over pebbles alternating with slate runs the full length of the Garden of Surprises, linking the Water House, a building furnished with water effects, to a tufa grotto at the lower end.

OVERLEAF This mirrored screen in the Garden of Surprises reflects on the opposite side the gnarled trunk of a old oak tree. On this side it reflects a water curtain and automata in the lower part of the garden.

The same effect is used in the grotto and the Moss House, where artificial light has a similarly shimmering underwater effect on their vaulted and domed tufa ceilings.

This use of reflection has been employed from the earliest times in grottoes - such as that of Emperor Tiberius at Sperlonga, and at Buontalenti's grotto of 1583-93 in the Boboli Gardens, Florence, where the light was filtered through a glass goldfish bowl suspended in an oculus at the centre of the domed roof - a source from above rather than below.

THE ALL-GREEN GARDEN AT SILVERSTONE FARM uses artificial light to give it an extra dimension at night. I like the reference this makes to the importance of lighting in the public pleasure gardens of the eighteenth century. At Vauxhall Gardens in London, for instance, ten thousand small glass oil lamps were lit simultaneously, this trick being one of the highlights of an evening visit. They were used to light the buildings, the orchestra stand, the supper boxes and the set-piece displays, such as the block-tin cascade. Today with cheap LED string lighting and pea lights, this sort of magical effect is available to everyone. The idea of outlining

OPPOSITE In the seventeenth and eighteenth centuries candles or Vauxhall lights were the prime method of lighting gardens at night. They were often used to outline the profiles of architectural elements or to mark axes. Here at Silverstone Farm they have been hung in the interstices of a large-spaced trellis.

BELOW Trellis obelisks housing simple spiked spotlights at ground level cast interesting shadows against the walls of this north-facing room at Silverstone Farm.

ABOVE The Green Theatre at Silverstone Farm. The curved hedge of hornbeam which forms the notional stage has arched openings housing urns. These urns are lit from the left-hand side at ground level by angleable spotlights hidden behind painted tin cowls. Side lighting has the effect of modelling form.

OPPOSITE The 10-foot flint obelisk is front-lit from a spotlight hidden behind a shell-shaped cowl. Front lighting tends to flatten out objects, giving them an insubstantial, theatrical look. In this instance it also highlights the texture of the flintwork.

architecture in points of light is an art form that has a lot of scope and a long history, though it is usually only done in Britain with any gusto at Christmas, when it often has great charm - perhaps one of the few expressions of folk art left in the country.

At Silverstone the Green Theatre is illuminated from behind its hornbeam arches, which form a stage-like setting for urns. In the auditorium, flaming balls on flint plinths are lit from inside, making the gilded copper rays stand out at night. Elsewhere angleable spiked spotlights are hidden behind shell-shaped cowls - making a reference to theatrical footlights. The great point of uplighting is that it is the direct opposite of daylight, making a whole scene look surreally different from the way it appears during the day. The night lighting of gardens should have a deliberately theatrical dimension - there would be little point in trying to subtly imitate the effect of daylight. By night it becomes easier to hide the more unattractive areas and make others more prominent. Experiment is often the way to achieve this, and a first idea of what is required can be achieved by the rather crude measure of moving large halogen floods - the sort that are described as work lights - about the site.

I also make use of the decorative possibilities of shadows, as in the way trellis obelisks with interior lighting cast a pattern of shadow against a wall, or by the close uplighting of flintwork to emphasize the texture of the pebbles.

AT WIVETON, an avenue of mophead *Quercus ilex* (see page 85) is at Christmas illuminated with pea lights, making a festive approach to the house, while to their left an oblong pool on the site of a tennis court is internally lit. Below this an open pool house with a fireplace in front of an oval swimming pool is lit for summer use as if it were a sitting room complete with open fire.

THE MARGINS OF THE SWIMMING POOL AT LOS MORITOS, TRUJILLO, are illuminated to take advantage of reflection. In Spain outdoor swimming at night is pleasant - in contrast to England where it is seldom warm enough. Here the grotto-like arches to the right are lined with rockwork. The small pavilion at the end houses a classical bust that is lit from inside the building.

OPPOSITE The swimming pool pavilion at Wiveton houses a changing room and storage, but is open at the front. It is lit by electric wall sconces and the glow of an open fire. At night these reflect in the oval black-lined pool. There are also flush uplighters at the bases of the wooden posts.

BELOW The swimming pool at Los Moritos is lit from its architectural surroundings rather than from inside the pool. The low illuminated niches set into the terrace of a raised pool room are treated as miniature grottoes. The small buiding at the end of the pool houses a lit classical bust. On the left urns and finials are set against a cypress hedge and lit from flush uplighters.

STRUCTURE

Congruity of style, uniformity of character, and harmony of parts with the whole, are different modes of expressing that 'unity', without which no composition can be perfect.

SKETCHES AND HINTS, 1795

THE STRUCTURAL ELEMENTS OF A GARDEN, both green and architectural, are crucial to both formal and informal gardens. They are the bones that hold a design together. As has already been mentioned, Repton had a very useful way of looking at this, an idea taken from picture composition, which was to create a distinct foreground, middle ground and distance to every view he formed. He was careful to point out, however, that painters' devices were not always suited to actual landscapes. The discipline of providing clearly defined foregrounds and backgrounds can be applied to gardens of all sizes and styles. It offers a creative stimulus to the designer, and to the viewer it gives the eye a way of 'reading' the scene, and adds a sense of progression through space as well as a sense of scale.

Repton would have categorized these broad spatial divisions as follows. Viewed from the house, the distance would comprise tree belts, individual trees and shrubberies, land forms and paths or drives. In the middle distance there might be a pleasure ground or a flowering shrubbery, park rail or ha-ha. The foreground might have a formal element: a balustraded terrace perhaps, or a trellis-enclosed rose garden or parterre. In some of his later works the formal element became more extensive, and sometimes houses might be provided with a formal entrance court (as at Uppark) or, particularly with houses in an historic style (he identified such at Penshurst and Knole), a sequence of formal enclosures, with an extensive series of terraces on the garden front of the house (as at Beaudesert or White Lodge).

In my work the formal element is more pronounced, and I have tried to think my way back to a pre-landscape movement aesthetic where formality might extend beyond the foreground into the middle distance, and even into the far distance in the form of avenues, formal plantations and view-stoppers.

LEFT The terraced gardens on the south side of Oxnead Hall lead down to the river.
OVERLEAF The formal geometry of the redesigned South Terrace at the Royal Hospital, Chelsea, relates to the axes of the building's main block and its flanking wings.

Repton's watercolour from the lost Red Book for Merly, Dorset, *c.*1795. It shows a treatment for the middle ground of the view - the detached flap below showing the 'before' scene. The idea is to connect the nearer hillside to the foreground park by removing its field boundaries and modelling its contour with carefully placed plantations. In addition, a view towards Branksome Cliff might be achieved by the opening up of the top of the hill. This is an unusual instance of Repton's depicting a panorama without framing it with trees into separate pictorial sections.

Nevertheless, the idea of retaining these notional divisions remains valid and useful. Where there is a mixture of the formal and the relatively wild, the contrast is aesthetically pleasing: the one adds counterpoint to the other. This is particularly pertinent now that the scale of private gardens has generally diminished, meaning that one has little control over the landscape beyond. Random planting seen against ordered structure can still be composed into a pleasing ensemble, and it is often the case that features outside your own control can be incorporated into the geometry of a formal layout, very much in the way that Repton advocated the 'appropriation' of a feature beyond his patron's landholding - as at Merly, Dorset, where in the Red Book he seems to be suggesting the 'appropriation' of Branksome Cliff in the far distance of the view from the house.

SOMETIMES THE ELEMENT OF FORMAL STRUCTURE needed can be quite slight. At Giffords Hall, in Suffolk, the main lawn within the moat needed definition, which was achieved with the insertion of an oak fence based on Hans Vredeman de Vries's engraved designs from *Hortorum . . . Formae* of 1583. Its outline is reinforced with a lavender hedge. At the corner of the

moat an oak open-work pavilion in the same style is planted with climbing roses. The simple geometry of these creates a formal link between the house and the yew-hedged formal gardens on the outer side of the moat.

This idea for what would, in the sixteenth and seventeenth centuries, have been called 'carpenter's work' is useful in that it can provide an instant year-round structure to immature hedging, as well as a clipping guide for forms that might otherwise be difficult to achieve. They can also be planted with free-growing climbers, as here. Carpenter's work differs from trellis in being generally heavier and simpler in design.

THE GARDEN AT SILVERSTONE FARM is divided up by walls, some previously existing, and by hedging in hornbeam, beech, yew and holly. In the initial stages some of the hedges were outlined in stout trellis to give the effect of height and structure while the plants were growing. The idea of the structural divisions was to create an interesting sequence of spaces leading from the house outwards. As the ground is almost flat the subdivisions have an important impact on the spatial interest of the site. I have tried to contrast narrow with broad open spaces, together with changes of direction, and at the same time to push visual axes (if not

Oak carpenter's work at Giffords Hall. The open pavilion marks the corner of a formal moat. Behind it the raised lawn next to the medieval house is framed by an oak fence in the style of the sixteenth-century garden writer Vredeman de Vries.

actual paths) to the furthest limits of a fairly limited site (about two acres in all).

As the garden is inspired by small seventeenth-century Dutch gardens (good models to follow for small gardens on a flat site), for the structure I chose primarily plant material available in that period: a fairly limited palette. For tall hedges hornbeam and elm were used, but given elm disease I have selected only hornbeam for the taller hedges, with pleached limes for added height – the latter sometimes in conjunction with lower hedges. Evergreens were an important part of these gardens, and I have tried to include all the (mainly Mediterranean) evergreens then available. The principal ones are yew, box, holly and native privet, with *Phillyrea latifolia*, *Rhamnus alaternus*, *Prunus lusitanica* and *Quercus ilex* as southern additions. The latter were much favoured in the period as particularly good topiary subjects, phillyrea making very good mopheads and rhamnus successful as a

trained wall shrub or as a pyramid or standard. In the period there were many named varieties of these two, some of them variegated, but today they are hard to find and I have not been able to locate any historic variegated varieties. Variegated evergreens were greatly esteemed as a way of introducing colour variation, particularly in winter.

AT OXNEAD HALL the garden is terraced down to a river and has some surviving walls and earthworks that already defined the separate areas. I added structure in the form of avenues and hedges, linking the main central terraces to the flanking areas and to the landscape beyond. To the east, separated from the main knot garden by a raised-earth viewing platform, I introduced a formal layout of hedges and lime walks, using a cross-path layout similar to that shown in John Adey Repton's 1807 reconstruction of this part of the seventeenth-century garden,

which he showed as a formal potager surrounded by planted arcades (see page 38). On the west side further avenues of lime have been added to extend the vista through a surviving sixteenth-century three-bay arched structure (also shown by Repton) towards the wilder woodland beyond. (This involved some earth-moving to level the main east-west avenue.) These east and west extensions have created two simply detailed formal areas that make reference to the original extent of the formal garden.

OPPOSITE, ABOVE These various forms of stout trellis at Silverstone Farm have been used to train hedging and to give structure to immature planting.

OPPOSITE, BELOW The more substantial niche behind the finial is planted with mature hornbeam.

ABOVE This lime avenue at Oxnead is one of several that lead out from the more elaborately formal main terrace.

THE GARDENS AT THE VILLA MARTIRES, TRUJILLO, are small but benefit from an extensive view of open countryside. The site is bounded by the battlemented defensive walls to the west and by tall walls on the town side. They also have to cope with dramatic changes of level as well as rocky outcrops in inconvenient places (see page 29). All these constraints, however, contribute to their interest. In the blistering summer heat some areas, such as the pool garden and an internal courtyard off the dining room, are shaded, while the main terrace with an open west-facing view is cooler in the evening. The owners have, over the years, made very clever use of salvaged stonework and ornament so that this new creation built of traditional materials already looks as if it has been there for ever.

AT MAS DES VIGNES FOLLES, BONNIEUX, in the south of France, a very simply detailed vernacular farmhouse set within its own vineyards, it was decided to create an equally simple formal area that makes the transition between house and vineyard. This is designed to create a sense of arrival and also to focus attention on the small entrance door at the junction of two ranges of building at right angles to each other. There are two low *Phillyrea latifolia* hedges framing the main buildings; these enclose a *boules* court with a new wall fountain at the centre of the facade. Four pleached limes also help to define the main block of the house. A tiny box-hedged forecourt draws attention to the entrance, and a few rows of lavender at right angles to the rows of vines give the only foreground interest needed considering the

OPPOSITE The pool at Villa Martires (above) is at the highest point of the site and is the only part of the garden to be screened from the spectacular view towards Portugal (below).

BELOW The courtyard at Mas des Vignes Folles creates a simple foreground to the view of vineyards and the distant hills.

grand sweep of vines and distant view of the Luberon hills that provide the main point of the site. On the other side of the house commercially grown lavender planted in rows comes up to the house and adds another dimension to the agricultural landscape.

AT BIGHTON HOUSE the garden was already sub-divided into a series of separate areas, some with long outward views into the larger rolling landscape. The Regency house has a charming approach with an early nineteenth-century Gothic *cottage orné* as an incident along the drive. The rest of the garden is quite structured, with a walled garden and planting by designers Xa Tollemache and Christopher Bradley-Hole. I provided the walled garden with a series of structures - two domed metal-framed pavilions trained with hornbeam to make green architecture and a timber classical pavilion. Elsewhere I introduced a new balustrade to the south terrace to form a Reptonian foreground from the principal rooms, with Christopher Bradley-Hole's yew cubes as the middle ground giving on to a panoramic landscape framed by mature middle-ground trees.

Sites often consist of a palimpsest of several eras, with the ideas of different owners and designers superimposed one over another. Repton often refers to this in the Red Books; he might be taking on a landscape by Brown or Emes or Richard Woods, his immediate predecessors in the field. Today I often find myself in a similar position: taking on and editing other people's work - or they mine. There are certain mid-century designers that turn up again and again at sites

where I have been consulted. I think in particular of Percy Cane, John Codrington and Lanning Roper - all very prolific designers with recognizable styles. John Codrington used Repton's before and after watercolour technique to illustrate his ideas. Percy Cane's three books on his work show how prolific he was between the 1920s and 1960s both in Britain and abroad. The net result is that a garden is hardly ever what Repton would call 'a creation' - in other words, a work starting from scratch, completed in one go by a single designer.

THE TINY LONDON GARDEN shown overleaf has been given a sense of theatrical perspective by the introduction of a series of trellis 'stage flats' in receding configuration. These trellis screens form the background structure to holly hedges and create a frame for a fountain at the end of the garden. They act something like Repton's idea of *repoussoir* trees - flanking trees that act as a dark frame to a view - an idea he took from the foreground foliage devices used in a painted classical landscape to throw the rest of the view into perspective. He used this constantly

LEFT, ABOVE At Bighton House, a timber octagonal pavilion has been built to provide a structure next to a newly made pond.

LEFT, BELOW A metal-framed pavilion is planted with hornbeam and flanked with hornbeam standards.

RIGHT, ABOVE This classical pavilion and seat create a focal point in one of the walled gardens at Bighton.

in his own watercolours - sometimes referencing earlier landscape painters such as Claude, Ruysdael or Watteau.

This theatrical garden is, however, inspired by seventeenth- and early eighteenth-century gardens where illusionistic perspectives were often taken directly from stage scenery, a connection reinforced by the contemporary vocabulary of gardens, much of which is borrowed from the theatre. In an influential work by John James, *The Theory and Practice of Gardens* (1712), a translation from the slightly earlier French of Antoine Joseph Dezallier d'Argenville, there are many direct and indirect references to the theatre - as in 'Halls of Comedy', 'Amphitheatres', 'Screens' and 'Shutters'. Another source of the vocabulary of gardens from this period is the nomenclature of the interior of a house - words such as *tapis vert*, *buffet d'eau*, *miroir d'eau*, *cabinets* and *salons* were all applied to garden features, further stressing the point that there was a

strong correlation between garden-making and the other arts.

It has often been noted - by Repton and others - that, paradoxically, the subdivision of a space makes it appear larger, because the eye is not easily able to gauge its real extent. In a small town garden this idea of receding screens set against the side boundaries has the added function of hiding the side views into neighbouring gardens.

BELOW Receding screens of holly backed by trellis give this small London garden a theatrical perspective.

RIGHT, ABOVE This garden made for the 1985 Chelsea Flower Show is an essay in distorted scale. Over-scaled foreground columns contrast with an under-scaled grotto and and low door: all conspiring to make a 15 x 20 foot plot look bigger.

RIGHT, BELOW A small, heavily shaded Belgravia garden has been given a trellis background backed by light-coloured paint. A reflective screen is set behind the lead obelisk fountain.

ORNAMENT

*There is no circumstance in which bad taste is so conspicuous, as
in the misuse of ornaments and decorations; . . . the landscape . . .
if encumbered by buildings in a bad taste, or crowded by such as are
too large, too small, or in any respect inapplicable, however correct
they be as works of art, the scene will be injured, and thus a thatched
hovel may be deemed an ornament, where a Corinthian temple
would be misplaced, or vice versa.*

THEORY AND PRACTICE, 1803

R EPTON WAS RATHER DISPARAGING about over-ornamentation, professing to prefer gardens where nature was allowed to take the lead. He was, however, a brilliant designer of a wide range of elegant decorative buildings and objects that, though sparingly used, were a key component of the pleasure grounds and the areas close to the house. Garden buildings, trelliswork, urns, fountains and seats were all designed in detail, often with the help of his architect sons, George Stanley and John Adey Repton, who were also interested in the house and its interior - not just in its relationship to the outdoors but also as a part of the creation of a whole aesthetic background for his clients. He would rearrange the plan of a house to suit his opinions on the best aspects for various rooms: an entrance hall should always face north, a dining room never west, for instance. The way windows frame a view was also important, and as an early exponent of the 'picture window' he suggested that windows be cut low to the floor to gain a view of a grassy foreground, for instance. Windows are generally, though, to be portrait in format rather than landscape - a view I share: it gives verticality and elegance to the architecture.

A flint niche in the orchard at Silverstone Farm forms a focal point.
The apple finials in the foreground were cast in lead from real apples.

TRELLISWORK AND CARPENTER'S WORK

REPTON WROTE that the masters in the art of *treillage* were the French, and it is true that the sophistication of French seventeenth- and eighteenth-century trelliswork has never been surpassed. A. J. Roubo's treatise *L'art du menuisier*, with section 4, 'L'art du treillageur ou menuiserie des jardins' (1775), a highly detailed pattern book that would be useful to any designer of trellis, might have been known to him. Repton often applied trellis to buildings. He provided inventive designs in many Red Books for alcoves, screens and entire enclosures of trelliswork. His later work reproduced seventeenth-century and early eighteenth-century ideas, as in the engraving of a trellis-enclosed formal parterre garden at White Lodge, Richmond, in *Fragments* (1816) which incorporated trellis alcoves at the corners and

arched entrances (see page 13). Similar use of trellis is seen in the Red Book for Beaudesert (1814), where historicizing parterres and flower gardens are shown enclosed by columns and fences of trellis with an entrance via a trellis tunnel.

Trellis and its rustic ancestor 'carpenter's work' provide a way of introducing architectural order to a design and are also a useful support for planting, both formal and informal. In the sixteenth and seventeenth centuries a garden could hardly have existed without being constructed around the bones of a carpenter's work frame. The designs of Hans Vredeman de Vries, published in 1583 as *Hortorum viridariorumque elegantes et multiplicis formae*, illustrate the way these oak structures defined the spatial layout of gardens. Being planted with hornbeam or elm closely trained

OPPOSITE A temporary trellis installation at Chenies Manor re-creates a seventeenth-century garden, with carpenter's work such as the Russells might once once have made here.

LEFT, ABOVE An exedra of trellis in the Garden of Surprises at Burghley encloses the water column, in which a gilded ball rises to the top on a hand-pumped body of water (setting off a random jet elsewhere).

LEFT, CENTRE Gothic metal trellis has recently replaced a long-defunct glasshouse at Prideaux Place, Cornwall. It complements other neo-Gothic features in the garden.

LEFT, BELOW The north side of the walled garden at Thenford has been articulated by baroque trellis and seats interspersed by topiary.

163

to the framework, they create a green architecture that has been a strong inspiration to my work. Contemporary descriptions and illustrations of these gardens make it clear how exact and sophisticated the results were.

At the Palatinate Garden in Heidelberg the mixture of real architecture and 'green' architecture was highly organized and made for a fascinating and rich effect. This garden, completed by 1618 for the Winter Queen, James I's daughter Elizabeth, was one of the inspirations for the Garden of Surprises at Burghley, as it was contemporary with James I's alterations to Theobalds. Both were gardens of compartments, each 'room' enclosing a different feature or centrepiece. At Heidelberg some of the architectural features are stone, with the rest of the structure in clipped and trained planting supported on elaborate carpenter's work frames, creating a rather surreal hybrid of real and topiarized architecture. At Burghley the garden is similarly enclosed by timber trellis screens stained a blue-grey colour, backed by hedges or screens of hornbeam, yew or lime (see page 120). At the entrance the complicated gateway in hornbeam is framed in metal trellis, which allows for a lighter, more detailed structure than could be achieved in wood.

LEFT, ABOVE A temporary pavilion of trellis, put up for the summer at Silverstone Farm.

LEFT, CENTRE Beds enclosed with stout trellis fencing mark out the effect of hedges before they have grown to maturity.

LEFT, BELOW A carpenter's work niche frames a plywood basket of foliage.

RIGHT, ABOVE On the south-facing terrace at Wiveton, we installed Regency iron verandah fragments and extended them to make a pergola big enough to dine under.

RIGHT, BELOW The view from the terrace is framed by metal trellis obelisks.

URNS AND SCULPTURAL ORNAMENT

BELOW The black-lined canal swimming pool at Silverstone Farm has at one end a fountain housed in a flint column, backed by hedges of *Rhamnus alaternatus* and yew.

OPPOSITE, ABOVE An early stage of the Theatre Garden at Silverstone Farm, with finials on trellis columns. The forest chairs, arranged in a curve, are copied from an eighteenth-century chair found at Uppark. Green-painted Windsor chairs of this type were the the ubiquitous garden seat of the eighteenth century.

OPPOSITE, BELOW This urn, made for me by Ivan Mapplesden, is copied from one made by Vincenzo Scamozzi.

THE CLASSICAL URN and urn-shaped finial are forms capable of endless variation and are a motif I have extensively employed - designing my own versions, sometimes using antique examples as a model. They appear constantly in Repton's work, either as a focal point or view-stopper in a pleasure ground or as a full stop on a balustraded terrace.

In my own garden I have developed several models from antique examples. Perhaps my favourite is one derived from Vincenzo Scamozzi (1548-1616). I have scaled it down and designed different decorative finials - some star-shaped, some with a notional representation of metal flames and others with a ball. They were originally created for the Grosvenor House Antiques Fair, for which I designed the architectural setting from 1994 to 2006. Also in my garden are lead finials copied from an original belonging to Charles and Sara Fenwick (whose garden features on pages 68, 69 and 182) and made by Brian Turner, a Norfolk leadworker who has an encyclopaedic knowledge of the history of leadwork and is able to cast new versions from old models.

The nineteenth century produced many attractive campagna-shaped urns. A pair of cast examples are sited on timber plinths on the south-facing terrace in front of my house. This simple fluted model, given to me by Richard and Frances Winch – indefatigable collectors of garden ornament themselves – are two of a set of four (the other two are in their own spectacular garden on the north Norfolk coast).

Elsewhere there are cut-out urns and ornaments – especially effective when viewed at a distance. These vary from very plain silhouettes to those with simple applied low relief. The simpler and bolder the relief, the more effective the illusion of three dimensions when the viewer is at a distance (see pages 172 and 199). This kind of illusionism comes from the baroque period, when effect was all and the means employed to achieve it less important. The visual sources for this sort of trickery are slightly obscure, but Kip and Knyff's engraved bird's-eye views reward close scrutiny, as do the many published views of Dutch merchant gardens on the rivers Vecht, Amstel and Rhine (such as *De Vechtstroom*, various editions from *c.*1730, *Rhynlands Fraaiste Gexichten*, 1732, and *Hollands Arcadia, Of de vermaade Rivier den Amstel*, *c.*1730). These early eighteenth-century engravings are a great source of information and inspiration for anyone interested in formal gardens.

Diarists of the seventeenth and early eighteenth centuries also comment whenever an illusion is particularly clever or, in the case of John Evelyn, if they find gardens going too far in that direction: 'my abhorrency of those painted and formal projections of our Cockney Gardens and plotts, which appear like gardens of paste board and March pane, and smell more of paynt than of flowers and verdure' (letter to Sir Thomas Browne, 1657, quoted in Evelyn's *Diaries*).

ABOVE, FROM LEFT TO RIGHT A version of the Scamozzi urn with a gilded cast-lead, star-shaped finial; a lead urn adapted from an old model, made for me by Norfolk leadworker Brian Turner; the finial on this urn is adapted from a wrought-iron finial on a sixteenth-century Italian urn.

OPPOSITE, CLOCKWISE FROM TOP LEFT A timber rusticated obelisk at Silverstone Farm; a wall plaque in timber, steel and copper at Blenheim House; shellwork above the pool pavilion fireplace at Wiveton; a wall fountain at Silverstone: the lead spout emits into a brick-faced basin with an inset cast-stone festoon; a terracotta bust of Ceres housed in a plywood niche with plywood frostwork pilasters.

POTS AND PLANT CONTAINERS

REPTON DESIGNED AND INVENTED a variety of decorative containers. Perhaps his signature planter is the basket – as in his giant timber 'Hardenberg' basket, for which a design by John Adey Repton survives, or as a fixed bed edging or, on a smaller scale, actual baskets see page 118). He also used green painted coopered tubs, plain terracotta pots, trellis plant stands and planted urns, all of which formed decoration important to the foreground scene.

The best choices for containers are tough and permanent plants that require only minimal watering and have an effect all year round. Such plants as sempervivum, ivy and phormium all fit the bill, depending on the size of the pot to be filled. These can be pretty much left to their own devices. If some watering is forthcoming, pelargoniums, helichrysum, bacopa, and *Erigeron karvinskianus* offer a long summer season without too much input. More difficult subjects should be avoided.

A collection of a single species makes an interesting if short-lived display, and I use plant stands or an auricula theatre to show them off as a group. This works particularly well with plants that flower in spring, when there is not much else in the flower border to attract attention: snowdrops, muscari, violets and laced primulas, for instance.

Larger, more architectural timber cases of the Versailles type can have a big impact in themselves, particularly as a repeat element on a terrace or to pace a design. This standard design can be varied endlessly, and I have produced wooden cases ranging from simple horizontal boarded versions to more elaborate lead-clad or panelled and framed ones. They generally look best when over 2 feet square, with proportions that are slightly vertical of cubic. The colour should relate to the setting but usually quieter colours are preferable, from grey to dull grey-green or dark green. Off-white or stone colour is also an attractive option.

RIGHT A view from Repton's cottage at Hare Street, after improvement (1816). The plant stand on the left hides haunches of meat hanging outside the butcher's shop opposite. Repton managed to acquire a small piece of land, once the village green, to create a simple middle ground to the view.

ABOVE The auricula theatre built into a curved corner of the walled garden at Thenford is axised on one of the cross paths.

RIGHT, ABOVE The plant stand just inside the gate at Silverstone Farm was made following a detailed design by Repton.

RIGHT, CENTRE Oak barrels painted Farrow & Ball Green Smoke and planted with *Phillyrea latifolia* standards.

RIGHT, BELOW Simple boarded Versailles cases in the foreground contrast with more elaborate framed ones in the background.

GARDEN FURNITURE

This similitude might be extended to all the articles of furniture, for use or ornament in an apartment, comparing them with the seats, and buildings, and sculpture, appropriate to a garden. Thus the pleasure-ground at Woburn requires to be enriched and furnished like its palace.

FRAGMENTS, 1816

REPTON WAS VERY INTERESTED in the way that a garden is furnished, and in company with his predecessors he favoured the use of green-painted Windsor-type chairs of various patterns as the main movable garden seating. One is shown in the front garden of his own cottage at Hare Street, and they appear often in Red Books. This was not the only type of seat he recommended, and his Red Books are littered with inventive designs for alcove seats, tree seats and benches. Both his architect sons provided designs for simple, elegant seats, often employing trellis as a motif. As a designer concerned with the overall look of a garden and with a strong interest in architecture and interiors, Repton realized that the character of furniture had to be in keeping with both the style of architecture and the type of landscape – whether formal or rustic.

Examples of historic garden furniture from pattern books and surviving pieces provide a rich resource. Often the period of a house has been the starting point for a particular design. At Penshurst Place, in Kent, I designed a pair of oak-panelled back settles, based on the existing fixed early seventeenth-century benches in the open ground floor of the King's Tower, outside which they stand.

At Thornhill Park, I used one of Sir James Thornhill's own sketches as the source for a pair of benches for a formal garden that was largely created by its recent owner, Tommy Kyle. For the same site I also produced another design that was composed of baroque scrolls and trellis with a half-urn as a finial. The leading characteristic of garden furniture of the seventeenth and eighteenth centuries is a bold and striking outline that makes a strong focal point easily read from a distance. There are many surviving carved seats of seventeenth-century Dutch origin that provide useful patterns.

A seat with a simple cut-out urn finial, deliberately simplified to read at a distance.

TOP, LEFT A baroque bench designed in the style of the early eighteenth century.

TOP, RIGHT This oak seat at Penshurst was designed to go with the seventeenth-century fixed seating in the King's Tower behind.

ABOVE, LEFT A seat I designed for Thornhill Park, after a sketch by Sir James Thornhill.

ABOVE, RIGHT A cut-out bench based on the *sgabello* benches often seen in the courtyard loggias of Italian houses.

Over the years I have produced many variants on the Italian *sgabello* chair and bench: a type of hall seat designed for entrances or open loggias which was usually of a simple cut-out design, painted to look three-dimensional and often carrying a painted coat of arms. The classic English Palladian hall seat is inspired by these Italian Renaissance and baroque models and was intended to conjure up the idea of an Italian interior. Since there are still so many of these seventeenth- and eighteenth-century benches left in Italian houses there is plenty of inspiration, and they show an inventive use of outline and scale. At the Palazzo Barbaro, Venice, the hall seats, still *in situ*, are about 10 feet high with a complicated fretted outline. The seats in this style in my own garden have simple bas-relief detail rather than *trompe l'oeil* painting.

The painted Windsor chair is still an excellent movable garden seat. Modern plain hoop-back Windsor chairs painted dark green with an eggshell finish look good. They can be assembled into a large set, not

necessarily exactly matching, since the paint unifies them. The ones I use at home come from an eighteenth-century model from Uppark, which at the time might have been called a 'forest chair' rather than a Windsor chair. Forest chairs are light comb-backed chairs of the type depicted in many eighteenth-century outdoor portraits (the painter Arthur Devis was a specialist in using them as a prop). Old ones are a rare survival.

Interior furniture forms generally have to be scaled up and made more substantial for outdoor use. The mere fact of being in the open air renders flimsy the slight and elegant forms that look well indoors. The benches with scrolled arms in the style of William Kent which I designed for the Christie's Sculpture Garden at the Chelsea Flower Show in 1999 are substantial, all their components being much thicker than their interior counterparts.

The eighteenth-century scrolled panelled benches of sofa form that survive at Houghton Hall are similarly overscaled, in order to work

in the grand setting of the hall and its large-scale formal landscape. The large armchair-like benches with cut-out baluster backs based on French eighteenth-century designs in my own garden are similarly bold enough to have impact from a distance.

In some settings the elaborate shapes of the rococo style are effective - especially where the furniture forms the principal object in a scene. I have produced several of this type all inspired by mid-eighteenth-century originals. They do not necessarily need the elaborate carving of their prototypes, and I have sometimes aimed to produce the effect of ebullient richness using fretted plywood and built-up layers of flat timber shapes to conjure up illusionistic three-dimensional form. This theatrical method - in the spirit of the stage prop - seems appropriate to the whimsicality inherent in the rococo style.

Sometimes garden furniture needs to be very plain and self-effacing, and in this case simple architectural forms work well, either as low-built walls at seat height (about 18 inches) or benches of plank construction. Such seating needs to be integrated into the design of the garden at an early stage. The simple stone benches with cut-out scroll ends that punctuate the gardens at Versailles are a good model to follow, especially as a repeat element in the design. I have designed many versions of this pattern in oak, stone and cast stone. The shape can be varied to fit and articulate a layout, curved or U-shaped sections being particularly useful.

OPPOSITE, CLOCKWISE FROM TOP LEFT
A seat at Kettle Hill incorporates an *œil de bœuf* window to give a glimpse of the walled garden beyond; a baroque-shaped bench at Blenheim House; a sofa-shaped bench at Bighton; baluster-back chairs based on eighteenth-century French prototypes; a flat-painted oak *sgabello* bench at Albemarle House.

ABOVE, LEFT Scrolled-end benches in the manner of William Kent, originally made for the Chelsea Flower Show, now at Silverstone.

ABOVE, RIGHT At Silverstone, a bench with frostwork edging, stained blue/grey.

Ancient Roman gardens such as the survivals at Pompeii and Herculaneum are another good source for these simple bench seats, and some carbonized timber examples have survived from the eruption of Vesuvius in AD 79.

Garden tables likewise can either be of fixed architectural form or light and movable. Again, the situation determines the type. On an open terrace near to a house it is useful to be able to rearrange furniture for summer, and light construction of wood or metal is probably the most useful; in a more distant spot, fixed furniture can be more massive, in stone, marble or cast material. Fixed console tables in stone look well when integrated into a design - in the niches of a wall or hedge, for instance. They also work well as pairs (as they do inside a house). There are numerous classical models from antiquity that provide inspiration. They do not have to be complicated or expensive (as the one cut out of railway sleepers in my own garden shows).

OPPOSITE, ABOVE At Silverstone, a simple console table made from old railway sleepers.

OPPOSITE, BELOW Plant staging made from landscaping timber stained grey.

LEFT A garden table on trestles, with benches made from landscaping timber.

BELOW A set of furniture in painted hardwood made for the trellis arbour at Albemarle House.

FENCES AND GATES

If the entrance-gate be wood, it should for the same reason [visibility],
be painted white, and its form should rather tend to shew its
construction, than aim at fanciful ornament of Chinese, or Gothic.

THEORY AND PRACTICE, 1803

REPTON WAS INTERESTED in all the decorative and functional aspects of a garden and landscape and paid particular attention to fences and gates. He sometimes provided designs and was concerned that the character, material and colour be in keeping with the setting. He could suggest anything from the most rustic split chestnut pale for a rural position to a light iron structure for an elegant villa. One of the earliest surviving structures is a charming field gate shown in his watercolour of Stratton Strawless, Norfolk (1780s). A similar gate survives from this site in the Museum of Rural Life at Gressenhall, Norfolk, in the form of a trophy of farming implements - not unlike the tailpieces in his published works, which show trophies of the landscape gardener's tools. Sometimes Repton would provide a client with a dimensioned sketch for a paling: the palings in my own garden are copied from one of these, painted in Repton's approved 'disappearing' dark green.

I have been inspired, in particular, by the idea of a gate made from garden tools, and have made many in a variety of sizes, from wide field gates to small gates for gardens. Old garden or farm tools of interesting shapes can be selected to put together a satisfying composition. Painting or staining them a single colour helps to unify them visually. Such gates need to have a plain background with simple posts - preferably in a hedge - to set off their complexity.

Much attention has been paid in the past to the design of fences and gates, and many have been illustrated in contemporary views - so inspiration is readily to hand. A book that has given me particular pleasure and information on this subject - and on many others relating to houses and gardens - is John Harris's *The Artist and the Country House* (1979), which catalogues changing taste in British gardens and their detailing from 1540 to 1870. There are also numerous pattern books from the seventeenth to the nineteenth centuries ready to be ransacked for ideas. In the United States good patterns of timber fencing and gates are still much in evidence

A gate made from a trophy of garden tools, at Silverstone Farm.

- and again are well documented in paintings and prints, and especially well represented in the reconstructed gardens of Colonial Williamsburg. Particular patterns of fencing also suggest the sort of gate appropriate to them, whether timber or metal, and I have produced many designs for both, some plain and some more decorated.

The traditional metal park rail consisting of four or five horizontal bars, the top one usually round in section, is late eighteenth or early nineteenth century in origin. Various patterns for different functions were available - a high version for deer, lower for cattle and sheep, and a denser pattern wired at the lower level for keeping rabbits out of the pleasure ground. Early nineteenth-century ironworkers' catalogues had varied designs for gates and their piers, which offer attractive prototypes. I have designed a number of variants on these.

AT HIGHAM PLACE, SUFFOLK, I reused old panels of park rail and designed new piers and gates to go with them. They divide up the various areas of the garden and separate the park from the garden. Being light in character and usually painted a dark colour, they have a minimal visual impact on the landscape picture as a whole. Such gates can, however, be sufficiently

BELOW Park rail with specially designed metal trellis piers and gates, at Higham Place.

OPPOSITE, ABOVE A pattern of standard timber palings copied from a dimensioned Repton design for park paling. it is painted dark blue-green - what Repton might have called 'invisible green'.

OPPOSITE, BELOW Pedestrian gates to the front door at the Red House.

RIGHT A gate designed
by Humphry Repton for
Brandsbury, 1789.

OPPOSITE, ABOVE The
elaborate entrance court to
the Warren house.

OPPOSITE, BELOW Chinese
Chippendale fencing and
Gothic gateways in the rose
garden at Warren.

decorated to make a statement at an entrance, as at
Tilbury Hall (see page 92, top) where they mark the
main entrance to the house through the arch of a new
stable block.

WHERE NEW ENTRANCE GATES ARE NEEDED in old
piers or walls, style and design are dictated by what
remains of the piers, which usually show whether
the gates were originally iron or wood. At the Old
Hall, Aylsham, there is an early eighteenth-century
painting showing the original timber gates. These
had been replaced by metal ones, probably in the
early nineteenth century. I was able to design timber
gates in the style of the originals adapted to the height
of the later brick piers. Being solid, they gave greater
privacy from the road, and they were more in keeping
with the late seventeenth-century architecture of the
house. (We repositioned the nineteenth-century iron
gates on the axis of the new pool and pavilion.)

NINETEENTH-CENTURY IRON-FOUNDERS' CATALOGUES
were full of simple patterns to enliven gates and gate
posts. Bosses and paterae were also cast in iron to
ornament solid timber gates or to be applied at the
junctions of iron gates. There are endless possibilities
here: sometimes casting a real object such as an apple
or a pine cone creates an interesting finial. Modelled
artichokes, acorns or balls scaled up and cast in lead
or iron offer further possibiities.

THE GARDEN IN WARREN, CONNECTICUT, shown
opposite is approached from a very small country
lane, and in this case the rule that approaches should
be given a low-key treatment at the road has been
broken to make a rather startlingly surreal entrance
court visible to all. The drive passes through this
to enter a vineyard on the left and a fenced rose
garden on the right. The inspiration for this slightly
incongruous rococo confection came from the film

designer Van Nest Polglase, principal set designer
for RKO studios in the 1930s. He paid close attention
to garden settings in movies, and in an era when
the baroque and rococo were newly fashionable,
the strong outline of these curvy and dynamic
styles had a particularly good effect on black and
white film. This garden turned into something of a
pattern book of the fretted-out fence, and different
designs proliferate throughout the garden – on stair
rails, round the swimming pools and enclosing the
different parts of the site (see pages 192 and 193).

AT ALBEMARLE HOUSE, VIRGINIA, I added brick
and stone piers in the style of existing ones at
the entrances to frame the central view from the
forecourt of the house. Cast gilded lead flames were
added to give a baroque presence (see page 41).

IN MY OWN GARDEN various patterns of wooden gate
have been devised to create entrances between the
various compartments. One pair set into a flint wall
with wiggly cut-out balusters based on seventeenth-
century staircase balustrades gives liveliness to a
see-through gate. Elsewhere a substantial oak trellis
gate is set into a hornbeam hedge to mark the axis
through the hedge.

LEFT A gate at Silverstone Farm copied from an American
painting of a garden of *c*.1800.

RIGHT, ABOVE The oak entrance gates at Friston have been
stained pale grey.

RIGHT, BELOW Wiggly baluster gates at Silverstone Farm. They
are painted Farrow & Ball French Grey.

BUILDINGS

It is not sufficient that a building should be in just proportion with itself;
it should bear some relative proportion to the objects near it.

THEORY AND PRACTICE, 1803

R EPTON SAW BUILDINGS AND GARDENS AS AN INTEGRATED WHOLE, neither making much sense without being related to the other. To this end he quite often recommended alterations to the layout or look of a house as an essential first step to the organization of the garden. He certainly had strong views on architecture, and with the help of his two architect sons designed complete new houses, as well as garden buildings, balustraded terraces and substantial alterations to existing buildings. He had a taste for the sort of ephemeral garden buildings seen in Regency engravings and pattern books; umbrellos (a type of canvas structure based on umbrellas), striped tents, alcoves and verandahs all appear in the Red Books. In addition, there are designs for cottages, lodges, summer houses, glasshouses, temples, aviaries, game larders, cattle shelters and dairies, all of which are carefully set in the landscape to create a view-stopper or object of interest. Sometimes Repton recommended works to an entire estate village, particularly where it sits close to the entrance of a park. He even suggested, purely as an object in the landscape, the building of a fake church tower or spire where none was to hand, a hangover of earlier eighteenth-century practice and not really in accord with his ideas on 'rational' improvement.

I always look first at the relationship of a garden to its house, and where necessary may suggest alterations to a house to make it more engaged with the garden, or to look better as part of the overall garden scene. Often houses have the principal rooms with the best facade facing away from the garden, or have large drives and parking areas separating the house from the garden. At Higham Place, where the very attractive bow-fronted Regency entrance front faces the village green, no principal room faced the garden. In this case I reconfigured a jumble of service rooms on the east side and redesigned this elevation to create a large garden room with bedroom

An aquatint from *Fragments* (1816) showing Repton's
proposed Gothic pavilion for Plas Newydd, Anglesey.

above, both looking out on to a newly created walled garden made from a yard, and opening up a vista of new gardens beyond that (see page 69, left).

A similar situation was found at Blenheim House, where the best rooms faced the village street with no sitting room looking over the garden to the south and west. Here I converted a groom's room and scullery into a new bow-fronted garden room with French windows in the centre of the bow leading to a raised terrace. This made a light summer sitting area with good views and access to the garden (see page 74).

At other houses additions have given a better engagement with the garden, as well as providing more accommodation. At Model Farm, Holkham, a new conservatory/sitting room has been built to link the front part of the house with the service wing beyond. It improves circulation internally and also makes a link with the garden, with its tall west-facing sash windows and central French window (see page 49).

There are also ways to give the facade of a house a more garden-like character - something that Repton did at his own cottage with the addition of a canopied porch on trellis supports. I have designed similar porches at a number of places. At a garden in Briningham (opposite), and at the Gardener's Cottage, Thenford (see page 60), I designed metal Regency porches for the front doors – an idea that immediately adds a *cottage orné* character and provides, with the metal trellis, a support for climbing plants. In a similar vein the partly old, partly recreated metal trellis pergola attached to the rear of the Wiveton house, reinforces its early nineteenth-century character (see page 165).

The refenestration of a facade can also help link house and garden, an idea Repton used at several places, such as at Barningham, where the lowering of the glazing of the Elizabethan casements improved the engagement of the rooms with the garden. At Higham Place the introduction of low sashes and a central French window to the ground floor made the rooms much lighter and the views of the garden better.

Similarly, the addition of a small garden room at Mill Farm added interest to a blank ground-floor facade and opened a view to the mill-race (see page 70). Gothic-style mullions added to the Gardener's Cottage at Thenford made a 1930s house sit much more comfortably within the eighteenth-century walled garden into which it had been inserted. In a similar vein, in my own garden, the Engine House, which already had rather decorative cast-iron arched windows (for a prosaic steam engine shed dated 1864), has been given an early nineteenth-century look with the insertion of a Gothic-style half-glazed front door (see page 58). At Blenheim House the octagonal-glazed doors that existed on the front of the house have been copied as new French windows on the other side (opposite, below).

A symmetrical garden does not necessarily have to relate to a symmetrical house, and designers were clever and inventive in the seventeenth century in making old irregular houses fit into gardens that had axial vistas running through them. However, it was the near symmetry of the front of my house that attracted me to it, and in order to get something of the same effect on the opposite side I refaced the rear elevation to make sense of a jumble of single-storey extensions (see page 141).

ABOVE, LEFT A metal Regency porch added to the front door at Briningham. The galvanized canopy is painted in pale blue and grey stripes.

ABOVE, RIGHT Dairy Cottage, Norfolk: two cottages turned into a dower house. Simple trellis has been added to the entrance front.

LEFT At Blenheim House we added octagonal-glazed French windows.

PAVILIONS AND GARDEN SHEDS

There are few situations in which any building, whether of rude materials or highly finished architecture, can be properly introduced without some trees near it. (*Theory and Practice*, 1803)

FUNCTIONAL OUTBUILDINGS are an important element of garden design, and there is no reason why a garage, stable or garden store should not enhance the garden scene. Quite often they also provide a valuable way of articulating space or creating a sense of arrival. One way of doing this - a device I have employed at several places - is to create an entrance arch through an existing or newly added building. I designed the new stable block at the Red House with a central opening to frame a new entrance to the rear of the house (see pages 56 and 91), and at Tilbury Hall in Suffolk a new barn has a similar but taller opening which provides the main entrance to the property (see page 92).

PAIRED BUILDINGS, in the manner of eighteenth-century gate lodges, are also useful as a decorative device. Repton was sceptical about small twin lodges as houses for gatekeepers, since a family had to live inconveniently between two buildings. However, as a frame to a view or as a way of emphasizing an approach they are invaluable. There are twin timber pavilions in my own garden designed to look like simple seventeenth-century Dutch gazebos; these frame a necessarily misaligned vista between the house and the nearby barns (see page 25). At Tilbury Hall a pair of smaller garden pavilions in similar style, and linked by pleached hornbeams, creates a full stop to the formal garden on one side of the house and also frames a lead figure on the central axis.

Vertical sentry boxes, especially in pairs, will also effectively frame a view. They have rather the same impact as substantial brick or stone piers, but with the advantage over piers that they can act as small

RIGHT Twin pavilions in the Warren garden frame a view of Lake Waramaug.

OPPOSITE, ABOVE Paired sheds terminate the formal gardens at Tilbury Hall.

OPPOSITE, CENTRE At Silverstone Farm, a flint obelisk that marks the end of the south side of the garden is flanked by timber sentry boxes.

OPPOSITE, BELOW The swimming pool at Warren.

storage buildings. They are especially good to have in small town gardens where they can be included in the foreground to frame a view of the garden or at the end to provide a full stop. When abroad I draw (and preferably measure) sentry boxes wherever I see them, as every European country has different models - usually adaptable to wooden construction, even when the originals are of stone or brick.

THE UBIQUITOUS SHED should make an object in its own right. I have designed sheds in a number of different styles. What might in the eighteenth century have been called Carpenter's Gothic is characterized by a certain whimsicality, with a (not necessarily very accurate) nod in the direction of Gothic architecture. Timber construction lends itself to this type of building and makes it easy to fret out Gothic detailing originally designed for stone construction. An interesting roofline is key to the success of such buildings (and indeed the one feature that lets down most off-the-peg sheds is the roof - usually too low in pitch and with a weak overhang).

It is also quite possible to produce a simple classically detailed shed: it needs only attention to proportion and the right projection to mouldings - which can easily be gleaned from one of the very many pattern books of the eighteenth century that are available in facsimile. The timber buildings of Scandinavia are also a good source; this is a part of the world where the builders of the past have worked out how to pare down classical detail to suit timber construction.

LEFT, ABOVE A classical pavilion in a Suffolk garden.

LEFT, CENTRE The back of the pavilion has been treated as a rustic temple in barked timber.

LEFT, BELOW A rustic pavilion in a Little Venice garden.

A STYLE PARTICULARLY IN TUNE WITH REPTON'S ERA is the rustic. Here buildings are constructed in barked timber or gnarled trunks deliberately left in their natural state. They are often thatched with applied decoration of pine cones or with walls patterned with twigwork or cork. Repton developed a clever classicized version of this style in which pediments and columns are suggested using simple barked logs of different diameters. This style of building works best, as Repton suggested, in an informal wild setting. He often recommended that cattle or deer shelters be made in this way to ornament the outer areas of a park.

THE IDEA THAT A GLAZED BUILDING to shelter plants should look like a substantial structure rather than a flimsy greenhouse is not new. I have designed a number of such buildings, both for plants and to be used as garden rooms. The seventeenth- and eighteenth-century orangery is a very good model to follow: in England it was rather different from its continental counterparts. A plain brick or rendered facade with a parapet punctuated by three or more tall sash windows or French windows makes a very satisfactory building in itself, and is often very useful as a termination to a town garden or a view-stopper in a country one. I particularly like the miniature early eighteenth-century orangery in Suffolk shown above right: a charming essay in the type, with polychrome brick and baroque stone finials on the parapet.

RIGHT, ABOVE A small early eighteenth-century orangery in a Suffolk garden.

RIGHT, CENTRE A simple summer house in a Virginia garden.

RIGHT, BELOW A new cricket pavilion at Holkham Hall.

RIGHT, ABOVE The re-facaded bungalow at Wiveton was given a new zinc roof and French windows with external shutters.

RIGHT, CENTRE This addition forms an entrance lobby to a range of barns at Tilbury Hall. It is built to match the timber *berceau* behind it.

RIGHT, BELOW One of a pair of lead-roofed pavilions at Model Farm, Holkham.

OPPOSITE Domed copper pavilions mark the intersections of diagonal paths in the walled garden at Thenford.

AT WIVETON I redesigned a flat-roofed bungalow to look like an orangery by inserting French windows on its main front. The long shutters give it a seaside air and also make it more secure when not in use.

I built an orangery-like building at Tilbury Hall to terminate the walled kitchen garden. It has Gothic-style French windows and a slate roof, giving it an early nineteenth-century appearance. It is built of colour-washed brick painted a bluish pale pink so that it contrasts with the red brick garden walls (see page 127, top). Another building in the same garden was added to an existing barn to create a glazed entrance lobby and to link to the oak *berceau* or arbour that adjoins it.

With the coming of cast-iron construction in the early nineteenth century it became possible to produce light glasshouses of temple form or with more exotically shaped curved roofs. Repton and his sons designed several of this type, with the addition of iron columns, pediments and acroteria to liven up the basic ridge greenhouse form. I have designed metal structures using this idea at several places. The two lead-roofed tents at Model Farm, Holkham, are early nineteenth century in inspiration and are supported on metal trellis pilasters. The domed circular summer houses at Thenford are of copper and are simplified versions of French rotundas, some designed to house eighteenth-century terracotta figure groups, others open or planted in hornbeam.

FICTIVE AND TEMPORARY BUILDINGS

A small building to command views of the sea was designed and built in a few weeks, having been executed in London and sent down by water, so that it arose up suddenly and looked like the work of enchantment. (*Memoirs* published 2005)

CONJURING UP A BUILDING by theatrical and illusionistic means is an idea that has a long history in gardens. Sometimes architecture was created from cut and trained plants on a timber framework, as was fashionable in the sixteenth and seventeenth centuries. Sometimes a simple timber facade creates the illusion of a more substantial building. Such conceits make good view-stoppers; when seen from a distance their lack of real substance is not evident.

I have installed such buildings at a number of places. For the 1998 Chelsea Flower Show I designed a trellis tower, made in sections so that it could be installed by helicopter in half a day. It was designed to contain bird nesting arrangements of various sorts for a show garden titled 'The Birds' Buffet'. At Ashwell, I designed a Gothic facade to break up the line of a long wall close to the house. This was of simple construction, made in shuttering ply and sawn timber with quite strong relief, for a bold effect. Such constructions need to be simple and strongly modelled to avoid looking flimsy even if their fabric is in reality slight. At Higham Place a grotto-like facade originally made for the 1987 British Interior Design Exhibition from fretted-out shuttering ply has survived as a facade to a recess in a garden wall for nearly thirty years. Its frostwork rustication is conjured up by the simplest means. At Gainsborough's House, Sudbury, a temporary installation I did in 1988 to celebrate the bicentenary of the painter's death was based on the sort of garden architecture used in eighteenth-century stage scenery. It was composed of a series of

LEFT A trellis tower designed for Flora for Fauna's Chelsea Flower Show garden 'The Birds' Buffet'.

RIGHT, ABOVE A Gothic facade attached to a wall at Ashwell.

RIGHT, CENTRE A timber grotto originally made for the 1987 British Interior Design exhibition sutvives in the garden at Higham Place.

RIGHT, BELOW An assemblage of plywood structures at Gainsborough House, Suffolk, They were installed to mark the painter's bicentenary.

receding planes designed to add depth and interest to two viewpoints in this small town garden. In my own garden I have created a few fabric and timber buildings to be put up quickly for parties. One of these, a domed temple covered in yellow muslin, was internally lit at night, so that its semi-transparent structure took on an ethereal quality.

I HAVE MADE SEVERAL TEMPORARY STRAW BALE CONSTRUCTIONS; the advantage of this material is that one can make quite large structures quickly (even if the possibility for refined detail is limited). My first essay in straw was made for the green amphitheatre at the Stoke-on-Trent Garden Festival, 1987, and referred to Batty Langley's 1728 treatise *New Principles of Gardening*, in which he encouraged the incorporation of farming into the formal structures of gardens. The bales took the form of small paddocks of sheep, circular plantings of barley, wood piles and haystacks. Their whimsical appearance suited the theatrical nature of the Stoke grass amphitheatre, a popular feature of early eighteenth-century gardens.

At Holkham Hall I was commissioned to celebrate British Food and Farming Year in 1989 by constructing a large group of straw structures near to William Kent's obelisk of 1719. It was intended to make reference to Kent's now lost formal landscape, which formed the view from the south front of the house, but was swept away later in the eighteenth century and finally obliterated when Nesfield's terrace and parterres were made in the mid-nineteenth century. In the tradition of those ephemeral spectacles created in gardens from the sixteenth to the eighteenth centuries, this straw group was burnt as a finale.

Another essay in straw was a representation of Nonsuch Palace built in front of one of the meres at Combermere Abbey, where it was designed to be first seen by party guests who were arriving by boat, and later viewed from the house. At the end of the evening it was burnt to the accompaniment of fireworks, all reflected in the mere.

OPPOSITE, LEFT A large straw folly built to celebrate British Food and Farming Year at Holkham Hall in 1989.

OPPOSITE, CENTRE A decorated haystack made for the Stoke-on-Trent Garden Festival, 1987.

OPPOSITE, RIGHT 'Strawhenge' – a representation of Stonehenge in straw, built in Salisbury Cathedral Close, 1990.

ABOVE AND RIGHT A straw folly built for a party at Combermere Abbey. At the end of the evening it became the focus for a firework display.

CONCLUSION

THOUGH REPTON RECEIVED a mixed press in his own day, no one can deny that his four major works on landscape gardening have stood the test of time. By the publication of his last book, *Fragments on the Theory and Practice of Landscape Gardening* (1816), he was certainly the most prolific writer on garden design in England - perhaps in the world. And though the editions published in his own lifetime were de luxe productions with a limited circulation, the compendium of his four main works published by John Claudius Loudon in 1840 under the title *The Landscape Gardening and Landscape Architecture of the Late Humphry Repton, Esq.* brought his ideas to a much wider audience and ensured their continued influence right through the nineteenth century.

Sketches and Hints and *Theory and Practice* were republished in America in 1907 with the title *The Art of Landscape Gardening*, under the auspices of the American Society of Landscape Architects. Frederick Law Olmsted acknowledged his debt to Repton in the design of Central Park. Today many of Repton's manuscript Red Books are in American collections. All his main works are in print, and facsimiles of the original large format publications with their sumptuous illustrations are available.

I hope this book shows that many if not most of Repton's ideas are still relevant and applicable to the problems facing landscape and garden designers today. When in 1982, with Patrick Goode and Kedrun Laurie, I organized the first exhibition on Repton, Sylvia Crowe, Lanning Roper and Geoffrey Jellicoe, at our invitation, wrote statements for the catalogue outlining his continuing contemporary significance. Sylvia Crowe concluded that his ideas for large private parks had application today even in the landscaping of roads, dams and power stations - in fact, to the improvement of public landscapes of the largest scale. I hope this book illustrates that many of his ideas are also still adaptable to private gardens even on quite a small scale, as well as to the exploration of how to relate gardens, architecture and the landscape at large.

This trophy of implements hangs in one of the outbuildings at Silverstone Farm.

Bibliography

Humphry Repton, *Sketches and Hints on Landscape Gardening* (London, 1795)

Observations on the Theory and Practice of Landscape Gardening (London, 1803)

An Inquiry into the Changes of Taste in Landscape Gardening (London, 1806)

Humphry Retron with J. A. Repton and G. S. Repton, *Designs for the Pavillon* [sic] *at Brighton* (London, 1808)

with J. A. Repton: *Fragments on the Theory and Practice of Landscape Gardening* (London, 1816)

J. C. Loudon, ed., *The Landscape Gardening and Landscape Architecture of the Late Humphry Repton, Esq.* (London, 1840)

Humphry Repton's Memoirs, ed. Ann Gore and George Carter (Norwich, 2005)

Index